Disagreement

Disagreement

Bryan Frances

polity

First published in 2014 by Polity Press

Polity Press
65 Bridge Street
Cambridge CB2 1UR, UK

Polity Press
350 Main Street
Malden, MA 02148, USA

ISBN-13: 978-0-7456-7226-7
ISBN-13: 978-0-7456-7227-4(pb)

A catalogue record for this book is available from the British Library.

Typeset in 10.5 on 12 pt Sabon
by Toppan Best-set Premedia Limited
Printed and bound in Great Britain by T.J. International, Padstow, Cornwall

The publisher has used its best endeavours to ensure that the URLs for external websites referred to in this book are correct and active at the time of going to press. However, the publisher has no responsibility for the websites and can make no guarantee that a site will remain live or that the content is or will remain appropriate.

Every effort has been made to trace all copyright holders, but if any have been inadvertently overlooked the publisher will be pleased to include any necessary credits in any subsequent reprint or edition.

For further information on Polity, visit our website: www.politybooks.com

In Part II, much of chapter 7 is taken from Bryan Frances's "Religious Disagreement", forthcoming in Graham Oppy (ed.), *Handbook of Contemporary Philosophy of Religion*, Acumen Press (December 2014); and part of chapter 11 draws on his "Skepticism and Disagreement", forthcoming in Diego Machuca and Baron Reed (eds), *Skepticism: From Antiquity to the Present*, Bloomsbury.

For Margaret Frances,
with whom I never disagree

Contents

Stories

Introduction

In the summer of 2011 the USA engaged militarily in Libya, leading to the overthrow of the Libyan government. Some informed people think it was an illegal war, since war by the US government has to be approved by the US Congress, which didn't happen. Other informed people disagree, claiming that the military action was not significant enough to qualify as a "war," so it didn't need Congressional approval in order to be legal.

Some Christians believe that Jesus rose from the dead – quite literally. Other Christians think that, while salvation occurs through Jesus, all that business about rising from the dead is metaphorical or otherwise non-literal: he didn't really, *biologically*, come back to life after being literally dead. Yet other people – highly intelligent, sober, and reflective non-Christian theists, agnostics, and atheists, for instance – think that Jesus didn't rise from the dead either literally or non-literally.

Disagreement is everywhere and can concern just about anything. It might arise from politics, religion, ethics, sports, philosophy, history, science, entertainment, and business. Controversy is rife.

Or just think about disagreement in your own personal life. Elena thinks that she and her partner Chris should get an apartment near the area in which the two of them work instead of getting a cheaper one that involves a significant commute. Chris thinks otherwise. So, the two of them disagree. They debate the pros and cons of the matter. Elena thinks it's pretty clear that, given the details of their combined financial situation, the hassle of the commute, and other factors, she and Chris should live in the city nearby to everything they typically go to during the week. Chris understands everything she said, but s/he adds things up differently, coming to the opposite conclusion.

Maya thinks that her father had an affair with that neighbor Martha when she and her sister Danling were little kids. Maya tells Danling her reasons but to no avail: Danling is totally unconvinced. Maya is inclined to read the evidence one way, as being very strongly supportive of the idea that Dad had an affair with Martha, whereas her sister is inclined to come to the opposite conclusion, that the evidence is not so supportive. Why should Maya think that her reading of the evidence is better than her sister's for finding the truth of the matter? Why favor her own judgment over her sister's? What if she knows full well that she is no smarter than her sister?

Devin thinks third-trimester abortion is morally unacceptable in almost all cases. But he isn't culturally clueless: he is fully aware that there are loads of people who disagree. Devin's sister Irene is newly pregnant and doesn't want to have a baby now. She doesn't want to marry the father; or maybe he is no longer around. She has little money or other resources, she has little time to devote to a baby since she is still in college and has a part-time job, etc. So, the question of abortion has come up. She discusses her options with Devin. What if Irene thinks there is virtually nothing wrong with it, especially since it's an early stage of the pregnancy? What is Devin going to say to her?

Actually, there are two issues here: Devin needs to figure out *how to act* and *what to believe*. He needs to decide what he is going to *say* to his sister Irene. But he also needs to figure out what to *believe* regarding the moral permissibility of abortion. He thinks it's almost always morally unacceptable, but he knows that there are loads of people significantly smarter than himself who have thought about the matter a lot longer than he has and have not drawn that conclusion. (And of course he knows that some of the people who *agree* with him are smarter and better informed than he is.) At the very least, I *hope* that Devin knows that, because it's just plain true! What makes him think he and the people who agree with him got the issue right and Irene and the people who agree with her got it wrong? What advantage does he think his group has over her group? Or does he think his group has no advantage over her group – in which case why on earth does he stick with his view over theirs? If Irene is similarly aware of disagreement over the moral acceptability of abortion, then she is faced with the same questions on what to believe – and a bigger question on what to do.

Devin is faced with the same two questions – how to act, what to believe – if the views are reversed: Irene thinks abortion is immoral and she says she has to go ahead with the pregnancy. Devin thinks that this move will be disastrous for Irene's future and abortion is fine in her circumstances. What should he say or do about it? And then there is the prior question: how does he know his view is even right, given that there are zillions of very intelligent people who disagree with him on the matter? No matter which side he is on, he is faced with a big problem about how to behave and what to believe.

Disagreements are everywhere, in the public square and our private lives. This book is devoted to the question of what we should do when we realize that there are people who disagree with us.

As we have seen with some of the examples above, the question is of enormous importance, both in the public arena and in our personal lives. You may disagree with your parents about where to go to college, or whom to marry. You may disagree with your spouse or partner about whether to live together, whether to get married, where you should live, or how to raise your children. People with political power disagree about how to spend enormous amounts of money, or about what laws to pass, or about wars to fight. If only we were better able to resolve our disagreements, we would probably save millions of lives and prevent millions of others from living in poverty. If only.

Here are some questions that provoke plenty of disagreement:

Political
1   Was the US military build-up in the 1980s a significant factor in the dismantling of the USSR?
2   Did George W. Bush and Richard Cheney intentionally lie to the public when pushing for the Iraq war in 2002?

3   Historically considered, which party – Tory or Labour – has done more for the working class in the UK?
4   Is capital punishment a significant deterrent of crime?
5   Should our country go to war, knowing that we're going to end up killing many thousands of innocent civilians?
6   Should taxes be significantly increased to boost funds for environmental disasters now that global warming is starting to have a large effect?

Personal
7   Did Dad have an affair with that woman Martha when we kids were ten years old?
8   Should deadbeat dad get to walk his daughter down the aisle when she gets married?
9   Should we put Grandma in a nursing home or have her live with us for a while?
10 Should we raise the kids Catholic?
11 Am I an above-average driver?
12 Did Grandma love Mom as much as she loved Uncle Jared?
13 Should we move in together now or wait until our relationship matures a bit more?
14 Should we get an apartment in Manhattan or go with somewhere cheaper and just deal with the annoyances of the commute?
15 Is our next-door neighbor paranoid or just nasty?

Philosophical
16 Do we have free will?
17 Does God exist?
18 Did Jesus rise from the dead?
19 Is there an afterlife?
20 Is time travel really possible?
21 Is capital punishment morally acceptable?
22 Is morality just about the consequences of our actions or are there inflexible duties as well?

Professional
23 Will extra trips to the tables get us more tips? (Imagine people who work as servers in a restaurant debating this.)

24 Will we raise our revenue if we maneuver the tables around to fit one more table in the restaurant?

25 If we ask for raises, will we get them or just make everyone mad?

Scientific

26 Is there a realistic way to curb global warming before it produces massive disruption to the world economy and welfare?

27 Did the universe have a beginning? Even if the Big Bang really happened, might there have been a universe before it?

28 Were the dinosaurs wiped out by the effects of a meteor? Or was it something else?

Miscellaneous

29 Who had more influence over the course of pop music: Elvis or the Beatles?

30 Will Lady Gaga fade away or become a powerhouse like Madonna did?

31 Who will win the World Cup next year?

32 Was Babe Ruth a better baseball player than Ty Cobb?

33 Should he add more sugar to the recipe?

This book lies on the border between theoretical and applied epistemology. Theoretical epistemology is the study of the relations among and natures of a group of closely related notions: knowledge, belief, truth, evidence, reason, certainty, rationality, wisdom, understanding, and a few others. We will not focus on those highly theoretical issues. Our center of attention will almost always be on real-life disagreements and what one is supposed to do in *deliberating* how to react to the discovery of disagreement. For the most part we will ignore the most theoretical issues and idealized cases of disagreement (although we will not shirk them entirely).

There are two central questions to ask about disagreement, which usually arise in the following situation. You have belief B and come to realize that some people disagree with you regarding B: they think it's false whereas you think it's true. One question is this: after the realization of disagreement, should you continue to believe B? That is an *epistemological* question. The other central philosophical question is this: after the realization of disagreement, how should you act or behave (e.g., should you continue to act on the assumption that B is true)? That is a question for *ethics*, including politics, not epistemology. This book is devoted to the first question only.

Philosophy includes the study of what to believe and how to act. So, it's not surprising that philosophers have had some things to say about the topic of disagreement. What is surprising, however, is how *little* philosophers have said about it, especially the epistemological question. Philosophy has been going strong for well over two thousand years, so you would think that an enormous amount of thought has gone into the two questions raised above. You would be wrong. As far as I know, this is the first textbook devoted to the epistemological question, although Oxford University Press published two collections of research essays on it in 2010 and 2013: *Disagreement*, edited by Ted Warfield and Richard Feldman, and *The Epistemology of Disagreement: New Essays*, edited by Jennifer Lackey and David Christensen (I have an essay in the latter work). Unfortunately, those articles tend to ignore the cases of disagreement that pop up in real life – the cases that we actually worry about and even fight over, occasionally to the death.

Since the topic of disagreement is so new, it is hard even to figure out what questions we should be thinking about. The two central ones mentioned above are a good start, but they are ambiguous and require refinement. For what it's worth, I have written many essays on the topic over the last eight years, and every time I write a new one I come to think that my previous ideas were flawed in significant ways; and I have no reason to think the trend is going to stop any time soon. In this book I refrain from offering detailed answers to the most pressing questions regarding the epistemology of disagreement and stick to going over what I take to be ideas that will be most helpful in addressing those questions. This means that I end up not discussing some of the popular views in the current literature, as I think most of them are premature (e.g., the "Equal Weight View"). I include so many examples of disagreement in this book because at this early stage of investigation we need a trove of data in order to explore the topic fruitfully.

In Part I of this book I go over the basics of disagreement. The goal there is to give the reader a sense of what the main issues and questions might be regarding the epistemology of disagreement. Part I ends with a generous selection of "homework" questions for the ambitious reader. In Part II I consider the question of under what conditions one is reasonable – in several senses of that term – in retaining one's beliefs in the face of disagreement; it also includes homework questions. As I said above, since this topic is so new and in so much flux, I decided to adopt the atypical organizational strategy of merely *introducing* many interesting test cases, arguments, and conclusions: I don't defend the arguments or conclusions and I barely even address the views found in the recent philosophical literature. Instead, I supply the reader with the background necessary to evaluate the arguments and views to be found in the literature. For readers who are old hands on the topic, sections 11, 13, and 14 of Part I will be interesting, as will all of Part II.

Part I
Basics of Disagreement

The most important thing you need to do in this first part of the book is acquire a deep understanding of what may be the most important *questions* to ask about disagreement. With that understanding secured, plus a raft of test cases of disagreement to think about, in Part II you will be in a good position to look closely at some answers.

1

Genuine vs. Illusory Disagreement

Before one is faced with the question of how to react to a disagreement one needs to have discovered the disagreement. Usually, there is no difficulty: if you think belief B is true and I don't – I either think B is false or I have withheld judgment on B – then we disagree. However, often what *looks* like a disagreement is actually illusory: there is no genuine disagreement. Surprisingly, a great many apparent disagreements in real life are *merely* apparent. Consider the following:

1   Abortion's Moral and Legal Status

If Bo says "Abortion is wrong" and Po says "Abortion isn't wrong," they might not be disagreeing at all. It all depends on the details of the case. Bo might mean to say that abortion is *morally* wrong while Po is saying that it isn't *legally* wrong (both of them talking about the same country and time period). They may well agree that abortion is legally permissible and morally impermissible; so, no disagreement exists even though their *language*, the sentences they used, made it look like they disagree. Alternatively, they might agree that they are talking about morality as opposed to the law, but they mean different things by "abortion," with one of them including nothing but third-trimester abortion while the other includes abortions at any time.

In that story the two people, Bo and Po, were using one word ("wrong," or "abortion") with different meanings. Here is a slightly different kind of illusory disagreement, one in which the two people are using a word with *incomplete* meanings.

2   Led Zeppelin's Influence

I say to you "Led Zeppelin was very influential" and you say "No they weren't." Now, we *may* be disagreeing with each other, but we may not. Perhaps I was really thinking something like "Led Zeppelin was very influential in pop music compared to many other rock groups," which is completely true, while you were taking a much longer, more historical perspective, according to which only Elvis and the Beatles, among recent popular music artists, count as anywhere near "very influential." You might have been thinking "very influential" means competing with Chopin, Beethoven, Louis Armstrong, and the Beatles. I may completely agree that Led Zeppelin is not "very influential" compared to them!

In this case we weren't really disagreeing at all, even though our language suggested that we were. Another case:

3   Michael Jordan's Height I

We are arguing whether basketball great Michael Jordan is tall. I say he is and you say he isn't. At first, it looks like we disagree. But then we realize that I mean that he is tall *for an adult male* while you mean he isn't tall *for a professional basketball player*. Naturally, when we discover these different meanings, we may very well admit that we don't disagree at all, since we agree that he is tall for an adult male but he isn't tall for a basketball player. Until you know what the "for" business is, you can hardly evaluate the sentence "Michael Jordan is tall": you have to answer the question "Tall *for* whom?"

In this case there is no difference in the meanings of our words – not even regarding the word "tall." Instead, we have different *comparison classes* in mind: the class of adult males versus the class of professional basketball players. However, the next story shows that, even if we agree that we are talking about adult males (so we agree on the comparison class), we could still be talking past each other and hence not really disagreeing when debating whether he was tall for an adult male.

4 Michael Jordan's Height II

Your standard for being tall for a certain group (e.g., the group of adult males) is something like "Taller than around 95 percent of people in the group," while my standard might be something like "Taller than around 75 percent of people in the group." Both standards are pretty reasonable (e.g., you can't consult a dictionary to see whose standard is best). In this dispute we are not talking about different comparison classes – the class of basketball players versus the class of adult males. We agree on the "tall for" bit. But we are still disagreeing about the standard for being tall. If we somehow managed to realize that we had been using the different percentage standards, then we would probably admit that we really weren't disagreeing about whether Jordan was tall. Instead, we would probably say that we had been disagreeing about what the word "tall" should mean.

That's a common phenomenon: two people seem to disagree about topic X only to discover, upon further discussion, that they are really disagreeing about what their words mean or should mean, the words they use to talk about X. A final case:

5   The Great Actress

Ugh, Mug, and Bug are debating whether Julia Roberts is a great actress. Ugh insists she is, saying that the fact that Roberts won a Best Actress Oscar award is all you need to know. Mug says he doesn't know what to think on this issue because he doesn't know what experts in acting think about her work; Mug is unimpressed by the fact that she won an Oscar award since he thinks such awards have little to do with acting talent. Bug is with Ugh, but for a different reason: he says the mere fact that her movies have made so much money is all the proof you need that she's a great actress.

Are Ugh and Bug agreeing with each other when they both affirm "Julia Roberts is a great actress"? Maybe not. When Ugh says someone is a great actress, perhaps all he has in mind is this: she has won the acclaim of her peers and other recognized judges of acting ability. That's certainly a reasonable way to fill out the meaning of "So-and-so is a great actress." But Bug might be filling out "So-and-so is a great actress" with this: So-and-so has successfully entertained a great many people. Ugh and Bug end up saying the same *words*, "Yes, she is a great actress," but they are really saying different things, at least at one level of meaning. It's not hard to imagine a situation in which Ugh knows nothing of the monetary success of Roberts's movies and also thinks that monetary success has nothing to do with acting greatness. In addition, perhaps Bug would say that winning awards is utterly irrelevant to acting greatness: the purpose of acting is to entertain, and entertainment success in movies is measured in revenue. Finally, Mug thinks that acting greatness is determined by the opinions of the people who study acting the most, perhaps the instructors at places such as the Juilliard School. The three of them are talking past one another.

We can even conceive of a fourth participant in the discussion, Jug, who conceives acting greatness to be determined by all the factors Ugh, Mug, and Bug focused on. Now we have four people spending an hour or so discussing a "single" question, but in reality there are multiple questions flying around; it may well be the case that each person is entirely correct in his or her conclusions, but the four of them never discover this fact.

Notice that discovering that there is no real disagreement might take considerable time; it's not as though the discovery will always be revealed in a minute or so. In the abortion case, Po and Bo might argue for quite a while, talking past each other for hours, before they figure out that they are using "wrong" in two ways: legal and moral. I have witnessed this happen on multiple occasions in my role as a teacher. The same holds for you and me with our fictional debate over the influence of Led Zeppelin, or the case with Mug, Bug, Ugh, and Jug.

In fact, in many real-life cases it's worse than that: Bo and Po may have started their discussion with *no real inkling* of the moral/legal distinction. But once they discuss things in a fruitful manner, they may, if they are lucky and persistent, finally discover that what Bo "really meant all along" is that abortion is morally wrong and what Po "really meant all along" is that abortion is legally allowed. But it might be even worse still: at the start of their discussion they might not have had any real solid view at all. When they used "wrong" they didn't mean morally wrong, legally wrong, or anything else that specific. They were just plain confused, as they hadn't really carefully considered the moral/legal distinction. And when people are that confused – which I think happens a lot: the Julia Roberts story is another real-life case – it can be extremely hard to discover whether there is any genuine disagreement.

Note, however, that it would be asking too much to demand *perfect* precision and understanding in order for there to be genuine disagreement. Suppose Sam and Pam disagree over whether third-trimester abortion is morally permissible in cases in which the woman's life is not in danger. There's no confusion over kinds of abortion: they agree that the method of abortion can be anything that is currently used. Nor is there disagreement about what the third trimester is or any confusion over legal versus moral permissibility. So far, it looks like a case of genuine disagreement. If a third party then pipes up and says, "But it's not a case of genuine disagreement unless they can agree on a strict definition of 'moral'," we would not be impressed with her objection. After all, who can define just about *any* word? Suppose you and I disagree about whether our cat is in the den. This can be a case of genuine disagreement despite the fact that neither of us can define "cat" or has perfect understanding of what a cat is. Similarly, we can disagree over the morality of third-trimester abortion even though we don't have a perfect knowledge of what morality is.

Here is another case, one that will look like the ones just discussed but really isn't:

6   The Greatest Baseball Player

Lee, Bee, and Gee are at a bar watching a baseball game and Lee asks, "Okay, who was the greatest baseball player of all time?" Gee replies with "Babe Ruth!," Bee replies with "Ty Cobb!," and Lee comes back with "Cy Young!" (Ruth and Cobb were hitters; Young was a pitcher.) And the argument is off and running, for hours on end – until the alcohol runs out, the money runs out, or the bar closes.

At first, this looks like a case in which there is no truth of the matter. One might think that "greatest baseball player" is too vague or ambiguous for there to be one true answer to "Who was the greatest?" After all, one person might value home runs very highly, in which case she will probably rank Ruth over Cobb (Ruth had 714 lifetime home runs while Cobb had 117). Another person might think that, since getting hits is the key, Cobb wins over Ruth (Cobb had a lifetime batting average of .366 while Ruth's was .342; Cobb had 4,189 hits while Ruth had 2,873). Yet another insists that pitching is the real key to the game, and so he picks Young over the others. Each of these "value systems" is pretty reasonable, and none is clearly the superior of the others. It's easy to convince yourself that there is no right answer here, because it all depends on what you mean by "greatest."

But this view – that there is no truth of the matter – does not hold in *this specific case*. It's true that there are lots of different intelligent and roughly equally good ways to weigh baseball greatness – no doubt about it. To that extent, the view of the previous paragraph contains some important truth! So I'm not saying that the view is worthless or lacks insight. However, the interesting thing about this particular case is this: no matter what value system you adopt in order to rank baseball greatness, as long as it's not a ridiculous value system Ruth is going to come out on top. The primary reason is that he is the only player in history to be excellent at both hitting and pitching – and he was *fantastic* at both of them. No one else comes remotely close.[1] In the story above, Gee really did have the right answer. (If they had been debating the question of who was the greatest baseball *hitter*, instead of *player*, then everything changes.) The lesson is this: *even if the disagreement concerns some vague, ambiguous matter that is open to several reasonable yet differing interpretations, there can be genuine disagreement and an absolutely true answer.* This shows how tricky things can get when attempting to discover genuine disagreement.

---

[1]Provided we ignore Josh Gibson and Oscar Charleston, neither of whom played in the major leagues as a result of segregation. But even they didn't pitch, so Ruth still wins.

2
Easier Questions about Disagreement

In order to understand the tougher and more interesting questions about disagreement, it's instructive to look first at the easier questions (which is not to say that they are easy!).

> **Q1**: Is it ever the case that two reasonable people can come to different yet reasonable answers to a single question?

Sure. This can happen when two reasonable people, call them "Pro" and "Con," have accessed very different bodies of evidence in coming to their contrary views. (Throughout this book, Pro believes claim B is true while Con believes B is false.) Pro's evidence gives strong support to B as the answer; Con's evidence gives strong support to not-B as the answer. Here is an illustrative story.

7 The Jury

During a jury trial in which the butler is accused of murdering the maid, the prosecution is able to present excellent evidence for his guilt but the defense is able to present equally good evidence for his innocence. Now imagine that the *only* information Pro has heard is the excellent evidence from the prosecutor – nothing from the defense attorney; Con has heard *only* the reverse. They aren't on the jury but the case is famous and they have heard about it via television and the internet. Pro has heard one side and Con has heard the other. Pro thinks the butler's guilty while Con thinks he's innocent.

Given that each side has truly compelling evidence, and neither Pro nor Con knows anything about the evidence that goes against his or her belief, each has a reasonable belief: "He is guilty" and "He is not guilty." Given that the butler is in fact innocent, Pro has a false justified belief while Con has a true justified belief.

Thus, the answer to Q1 is "Yes": when the two people have *opposed yet strong bodies of overall evidence*, then they can very reasonably hold opposite beliefs.

Q2: Is it ever the case that two reasonable people can come to different yet reasonable answers to a single question when they have the same data?

In the answer to Q1, I had Pro and Con have very different bodies of evidence. With Q2, we are attempting to make Pro and Con more equal by insisting that they have the same data to work with.

But, again, the answer to Q2 is "Yes," as another story will prove.

8 The Chemistry Class

Pro and Con are college students taking a chemistry class together. They are working on a difficult home-work problem. They are given the exact same data and are asked to determine whether the chemical sample will get over 200° Celsius during the course of a specific experiment. Pro has a great deal of background chemistry knowledge that Con lacks – background knowledge that is crucial for solving the problem. Because of that difference, Pro is able to figure out that the answer is "No," while Con goes down a blind alley and comes up with the answer "Yes." But Con has done nothing stupid or otherwise unreasonable. She just didn't have the one piece of background knowledge necessary to see that her way of solving the problem, although it certainly looked utterly straightforward, was mistaken. Con's solution is incorrect but reasonable enough to get a B grade on the assignment. Without having the key piece of background knowledge, Pro would have done the same thing as Con did.

Thus, two reasonable people can come to different yet reasonable answers to a single question when they have the same data, provided one has key *background knowledge* the other lacks and there is a reasonable yet mistaken way of trying to answer the question from that set of data.

> Q3: Is it ever the case that two reasonable people can come to different yet reasonable – in the sense of not stupid – answers to a single question when they have the very same evidence, including background knowledge and data?

With Q2 we had Pro and Con have the same data but have different background knowledge. With Q3 we insist that they have the same evidence, *including* background knowledge as well as data. So, we are making them more equal.

If by "reasonable" you just mean *not stupid*, as is made explicit in Q3, then the answer to Q3 is "Yes." An illustrative story:

9 Restaurant Bill I

You're at a fancy restaurant with friends and you get the bill, which comes to $215 including the tip. There are five of you at the table and you agree to pay equal shares. You know full well that you and your friend are roughly equally good at doing arithmetic in your heads, without the aid of paper, pen, calculators, etc. But, although both of you are pretty good at it, neither of you is *very* good at it. You both try to figure out how much each person owes, doing the calculation quickly in your heads. You get $43 while your friend gets $45.

(Based on Christensen, 2007)

Given that you both did the calculation quickly, it is not surprising that you got different answers. If you then put $43 on the table and she puts $45 on the table, then, although only one of you got the right answer, neither of you has done anything stupid or foolish. Perhaps you shouldn't trust yourself so much as not to get confirmation on what the proper amount is: maybe you should have checked with others before you put your money down. But are you being *unreasonable* in believing that your share is $43? Well, it all depends on what the minimal "bar" or threshold is for being reasonable. If the bar is pretty low, as in Q3, then both of you were reasonable; if the bar is high, then you were unreasonable. The lesson: we need to specify the notion of reasonability at issue when figuring out whether two people have "reasonable" beliefs.

One key thing to keep in mind: in this book, in which we are trying to figure out how to react reasonably to the discovery of disagreement, we are employing a notion of reasonableness that is stronger than *not stupid* but not so high that almost none of us ever meets it. I will return to this point later in Part I.

In the Restaurant Bill I story we didn't consider what happens when the two of you learn of your different answers. All we considered was the question of your reasonability *before* you discover the disagreement. What happens *after* the discovery will be the main theme of this book, especially in Part II.

> **Q4:** Is it ever the case that two reasonable people can come to different yet reasonable – in a sense significantly stronger than that of not being stupid – answers to a single question when they have the very same evidence, including data and relevant background knowledge?

The difference between Q3 and Q4 is that the former employed a very weak notion of rationality whereas the latter uses a stronger one (but not so strong as to be merely ideal or otherwise unrealistic). But, once again, the answer is "Yes."

10 Math Skills

Tyler and Marge are faced with the same difficult question, they have the same evidence, but Marge is mathematically gifted and Tyler is not too bright when it comes to math. For instance, Tyler and Marge are twelve-year-olds faced with a hard math question. Marge is just naturally proficient at math; Tyler struggles with even simple things such as "$51 \times 35 = ?$." They have received the same education: they might be twins who have had the exact same classes in school, the same educational home life, etc. They have been exposed to the same mathematical education and have listened equally attentively. Even so, as soon as Marge hears the math question she hits on the right answer, whereas Tyler does not. Neither Marge nor Tyler is terribly aware of the skill differential, as neither of them pays attention to such things.

It's not that Marge remembers some mathematical fact that Tyler is unaware of. This is not a case of differing background knowledge in the sense of a difference in *factual* knowledge. Instead, Marge just has a *cognitive ability* that Tyler lacks. You could categorize that difference as one in "background knowledge," but I am using that phrase for factual knowledge alone.

Since the math problem facing Tyler is so difficult for him, he can be reasonable in coming to a wrong answer. He gets the answer 52 whereas the correct answer, the one Marge got, is 42. Not only is Tyler's answer not stupid, it's quite reasonable given how tricky the math problem is for anyone who doesn't have Marge's abilities.

Now you might think that Tyler is being unreasonable here: he actually should suspend judgment. He should not come to any conclusion at all, let alone the answer 52. But surely this is asking too much of a twelve-year-old. How one's cognitive maturity influences assessments of reasonability is an issue we will take up in Part II.

Even if Marge and Tyler are equal in their long-term cognitive abilities, they might reasonably get different answers provided that one has an unknown *temporary* cognitive deficit. For instance, maybe Tyler is on some strong medication today that impairs his reasoning power, although he doesn't know this because his parents didn't tell him. He is generally just as good at math as Marge is, but today he is not up to snuff. So, when we say that people can come to different reasonable beliefs because they differ in cognitive ability even though they had the same data, evidence, and background knowledge, the difference in cognitive ability might be either temporary or long-term.

> Q5: Is it ever the case that two reasonable people can come to different yet reasonable – in a sense stronger than that of not being stupid – answers to a single question when they have the very same evidence, data, relevant background knowledge, and cognitive ability?

Q4 said that the two people are the same in data and background knowledge but failed to insist that they are the same when it comes to ability. Q5 says they have to be the same in relevant ability. So now they are more equal. But once again, the answer is "Yes"!

11   The Economics Class I

Consider two college students majoring in economics who are working on a devilishly difficult problem in one of their economics classes. They are equally bright, they have the same data, and they have the same background knowledge and ability. So they are equal in many relevant ways. The professor knows that the problem is difficult because she knows that, when her students first read it, they will be very tempted to tackle it in a certain way – a way that leads to the wrong answer. In order to hit on the right way to solve it, one has to think long and hard and realize that an alternative way is the right way. Joan works on the problem for thirty minutes. She adopts the "obvious" approach, the one that gives the wrong answer, and ends up with the answer X. Harold has a lot more time to devote to the problem. When he works on it for the first thirty minutes, he does exactly what Joan did: he goes down the blind alley and gets the same incorrect answer. But, unlike Joan, he goes back and thinks about the problem much more than she did. Again, he's got the time to devote to it and he sticks with it because he wants to raise his grade. Eventually he realizes that there is an alternative way to tackle the problem. And, when he pursues it, he sees that the alternative way is the right way and the "obvious" way was the wrong way. So, he ends up with answer Y, which is correct.

Both Joan and Harold have come up with reasonable answers. In fact, Joan's answer is worth a B grade, which is nothing to sneeze at. They are two reasonable people coming to different yet reasonable answers to the same question based on the same evidence, background knowledge, and ability. The key is this: Harold is able to put a lot more *time* into the matter – time that enables him to see things and think things that Joan does not see or think. You might even argue that these differences mean that, although Harold and Joan *started* with the same evidence, with his extra thought Harold got some *additional* evidence that Joan missed out on. He found some additional information relevant to answering the question, and so he ended up basing his answer Y partly on this piece of information – which Joan did not do. So, even though they started with the same evidence, eventually they differed in what they based their answers on. Later in the book we'll consider cases in which the two individuals, unlike Harold and Joan, base their opinion on precisely the same evidence.

Q6: Is it ever the case that two reasonable people can come to different yet reasonable – in a sense stronger than that of not being stupid – answers to a single question when they have the very same evidence, data, relevant background knowledge, and ability, and have worked on the question for a comparable amount of time?

Q5 said that the two people are the same in data and relevant background knowledge and ability but failed to insist that they are the same when it comes to time devoted to answering the question. Q6 says they have to be the same in the latter respect. But, once again, the answer is "Yes."

12   The Economics Class II

Reggie and Amanda are in the same economics class as Harold and Joan. Reggie and Amanda are equal in every relevant respect noted thus far: overall ability, relevant background knowledge, time devoted to the question, and data and evidence generally. But, whereas Amanda works on the problem without any annoying distractions, Reggie is surrounded by boisterous children vying for his attention.

Despite his best efforts, Reggie ends up distracted enough to come up with an answer different from Amanda's. They both did well in answering the question (e.g., they both get Bs, say); each ends up with a reasonable belief regarding the answer. Here the crucial factor that led to the reasonable disagreement was the *circumstances of investigation*. As with Q5, one can argue that Reggie ends up missing out on evidence that Amanda has, so they *started* but didn't *finish* with the same evidence.

What we have been doing, with Q1 to Q6, is discovering some primary factors – the **Disagreement Factors** – that lead people to divergent yet reasonable answers to a single question:[2]

Data
Evidence
Time
Ability
Background Knowledge
Circumstances of Investigation.

We also saw that there are different conceptions of reasonable belief: a belief can be "reasonable" under one conception but not another.

[2]Throughout this book, key terms appear in bold italics.

3
Harder Questions about Disagreement

It's time to switch gears. Now ask this question: what should you do when you *realize* that you disagree with someone about some belief of yours? In the answers to questions Q1 to Q6, each pair of protagonists was never aware of each other's beliefs. It was never said that one knew what the other thought or vice versa. But what happens when they do learn this information, when Pro and Con, say, realize that they have come to different answers? Disagreement by itself isn't terribly interesting; the *awareness of* disagreement is the worrisome topic.

Suppose you come to have belief B. It doesn't matter what B is; it can be any belief you like. Then you find out about Jones: she thinks B is false, whereas you had thought that B is true. Should this fact worry you? Now we are considering the question "How should you react to the realization of disagreement?" Call that the **Disagreement Question** (it will be made more precise in section 13).

There are several possible answers to the Disagreement Question. One is "You should stick with your old belief B." In that case, the appropriate thing for you to do is say to yourself that you're right and the person disagreeing with you is wrong. This would be the appropriate response if the realization of disagreement doesn't give you any good reason to change your view about B. Another answer to the Disagreement Question is "You should suspend judgment on whether B is true." This would probably be the appropriate response if the realization of disagreement does give you good but not conclusive reason to think that your initial belief was false.

A third answer is "You should adopt the other person's view and believe that B is false." This would probably be the appropriate response if the realization of disagreement gave you excellent overall reason to think B is false. Of the three possible answers, which is right?

On the face of it, the answer to the Disagreement Question in a given dispute depends in turn on the correct answer to this crucial question: *are you in a better position to judge B than Jones is?* Call that the **Better Position Question**. Roughly put, when you learn that some people disagree with you, you may well ask whether those people know something you don't know. As a general rule, if you come to think that they have some key information you don't have, then you'll be worried that your belief B is false; if you think that you know some things they have missed, then you'll probably think they are the ones who made a mistake. It's pretty clear that the answer to the Disagreement Question is often closely linked with the answer to the Better Position Question.

If B is a belief such as "Jupiter has twelve moons," then it's easy to see how the answer to the Better Position Question can be "No" and the answer to the Disagreement Question can be "You should adopt the other person's view."

13   Jupiter's Moons

You think Jupiter has twelve moons. You base this belief on what you dimly recall from elementary school; for a great many years now you have been far removed from science. Then you read in the science section of the *New York Times* that all astronomers hold that Jupiter has at least sixteen moons. You know full well that you're no astronomer, your belief is based on nothing but a dim memory from childhood, and the astronomers are clearly experts compared to you. You're not so arrogant to think that you know more than they do about Jupiter!

However, even though that case is clear, it needs to be mentioned that, when it comes to some scientific topics, a great many people are either unaware that there is a body of experts on the subject or they know it but refuse to acknowledge it. For instance, if one knows pretty much anything about science, one knows that there are experts on climate and experts on long-term biological change. The former group is quite large and has for many years insisted that global warming is real, primarily human made, and potentially catastrophic; the latter group is also large and has for many years insisted that the Earth's species have evolved over many millions of years. Despite those facts about expertise, many non-scientists have little or no psychological problem with dismissing those expert opinions. They will defer to scientists in some cases, but it can be much harder when the scientists are saying something they find uncomfortable. They don't care how many moons Jupiter has, so they are happy to defer to astronomers; they do care about the origins of humans and the vast changes to our way of life recommended by the climate scientists. In several places in this book we will take a close look at controversial beliefs.

Continuing our investigation of the Better Position Question, there are lots of instances when you should be *utterly unconcerned* that someone disagrees with you. In these cases the answer to the Better Position Question is "Yes" and the answer to the Disagreement Question is "You should stick with your old belief."

14 Marriage-Slavery

I remember a student once saying – and, no, I'm not joking – that he thought that being married to someone meant that one is a *slave* to that person. I believe he is wrong. I've been married about twenty years now, I know many couples who have been married for comparable as well as greater lengths of time, and the student in question was nineteen years old and unmarried. Quite frankly, he didn't know what the hell he was talking about, and for all my faults I do know what the hell I'm talking about. This is *not* to say that I'm a genius when it comes to the institution of marriage, or that I'm generally smarter than he is. It means nothing of the sort. Instead, think of some of the factors we looked at in the previous section: evidence, background knowledge, and time to reflect. I've got tons more evidence and relevant background knowledge than he does when it comes to the marriage-slave question; and I've thought about marriage a lot more than he has. It's just no contest.

This doesn't mean that when he and I disagree about marriage I'm *always* going to be the one who is right. All it means is this: I'm in a much, much better position to make accurate general judgments about marriage than the student was. My *epistemic position* with respect to the question "Does being married to someone mean that you are their slave?" is superior to his. As a consequence, when I learn that he says that married people are slaves to each other, I should not be too worried that I am missing something and have gone wrong in my opposite belief.

Here is another example.

15   Math is Stupid

Children occasionally complain about being forced to learn mathematics. Sometimes they think it's stupid that they have to learn something that they are never going to use in life. I completely disagree with that belief of theirs – in fact, math, logic, and philosophy are the *only* things I ever learned that *increased my ability to reason*, so I tend to value them highly. When I discover that such children believe the opposite of me, I am not in the slightest worried that I might be wrong. I know that I have a huge advantage over them when it comes to this issue, as I have been teaching and reflecting on pedagogical issues for over twenty years (and as I was writing this book I was confronted with a wholly practical problem whose solution required logarithms). As in the previous story, my advantage has to do with more evidence, more relevant background knowledge, and more quality time reflecting on the issue.

Evidence is a key factor: if you know that you have all their evidence *plus* some more evidence that is pivotal, then, provided you know that you don't have some special reason to think they have some other advantage over you, you probably shouldn't be concerned that your belief is false, just because they disagree with you. Here is an especially vivid illustration.

16   The Toothache

Suppose you have an agonizing toothache. You go to several dentists and doctors and they can't find anything wrong with your teeth or any other relevant part of your body. Eventually you generate enough interest in the medical community that the best doctors in the world spend a good amount of their time examining you. They still can't understand what's wrong with you. Then they find out from your spouse that you are seeing a psychologist because you have tremendous difficulty refraining from lying. "Well now!" they say. "That changes everything!" Now they say to you, "You *can't* be in pain! You're just faking it!" That is the majority expert opinion. You know only so much about pain and nerve endings. Even so, you do *know* that you're in pain. On the doctors' advice you might give up your belief that it's your *tooth* that's the source of your pain, but you insist – and know – that you are in pain.

The hypothesis that you aren't in pain is endorsed by the expert medical people, you have no special expertise about pain and nerve endings, you need to have some epistemically impressive item in order to be reasonable in sticking with your "I am in pain" belief, but you *have* it via some special experiences (the painful ones, naturally).

What is important about the toothache story is that it shows this: *there can be serious expert doubt cast on your belief, you are no genius in rebutting those experts, and yet your belief is reasonable anyway if it comes from experience in the right way*. However, as the oddity of the example suggests, this is going to be a relatively rare occurrence.

As stated previously, we saw various factors – the **Disagreement Factors** – that might cause reasonable people to come to reasonable yet contrary beliefs: data, evidence, time, ability, background knowledge, circumstances of investigation. (That is not an exhaustive list and the items aren't all mutually exclusive; it's just a good beginning.) These are also factors that can justify one in sticking to one's belief.

For instance, suppose Pro knows both of these facts:

- Pro surpasses Con in some of the Disagreement Factors.
- Con doesn't surpass Pro in any of those factors.

Pro can reasonably say to herself, "Well, I know Con disagrees with me here, but I'm not too worried that I'm missing something because it certainly looks as though Con is the one who is missing something." In those cases, the answer to the Better Position Question is "Yes" and the answer to the Disagreement Question is "You should stick to your old belief." At least, that is a decent rule of thumb; we will have to probe deeper to see if it's true in *all* interesting cases.

So far we have looked at instances of the Disagreement Question that have the correct answer "You should stick with your old belief" (e.g., the marriage-slave, toothache, and education-math cases) and other instances of the Disagreement Question that have the correct answer "You should adopt the other person's view" (e.g., the Jupiter-moon case). But it's easy to see that yet other instances have the correct answer "You should suspend judgment."

17   Thermometers

You're in a chemistry lab class working with a lab partner. You need to ascertain the temperature of the liquid solution you are working with. You put a thermometer in the solution, wait a minute, take it out, and read that it says the liquid is at 78° Celsius. You have no reason to doubt the thermometer is working, so you come to believe the liquid's temperature is 78. Just to be sure, your partner does the exact same thing, using another thermometer that, for all you two can tell, is just as good as the one you used. But she gets a reading of 83 even though the liquid is stable and well sealed, so that its temperature couldn't change that much in the space of a minute. Finally, she is your equal in general intelligence, knowledge of chemistry, and the other Disagreement Factors.

(Based on Thomas Kelly's "Peer Disagreement and Higher-Order Evidence," in Feldman and Warfield, 2010)

In this case it's pretty clear that you should suspend judgment on the belief "The temperature is 78" (and you should suspend judgment on "The temperature is 83" as well). You know that she checked the temperature just as competently as you did, and you have no reason at all to trust one reading over the other. So the answer to the Disagreement Question is "You should suspend judgment." Pretty clearly, you should get another temperature reading, preferably with another thermometer.

In the Thermometers story you and your lab partner could have differed in many ways: you might be much smarter than she is, or maybe you have a lot more experience with using thermometers. So you might have the advantage over her when it comes to some important Disagreement Factors. But notice that, in the particular case at hand, those advantages didn't matter! The task you both had before you – measure the temperature in the container – was so simple that your advantages in ability and experience didn't matter when faced with the question of which temperature reading to trust, if any. There are lots of examples of this.

However, what does it mean to "suspend judgment" on belief B? Roughly put, it means you do not believe that B is true and do not believe B is false. When you suspend judgment on "The temperature is 78," it's not true that you *adopt the other person's view*. If you start out believing B but then suspend judgment (also called "withhold belief"), that means you do not endorse B and you do not endorse not-B, even though you've thought about it. If you start out believing B but then adopt the other person's view, that means you do not endorse B but you do endorse not-B. Thus, suspending judgment is importantly different from adopting the other person's view.

In addition, suspending judgment does not mean "make my decision for me." I'm agnostic with regard to whether God exists, but the last thing I'm going to do is believe what some person tells me to do in deciding whether God exists.

There are two common kinds of case in which we should suspend judgment. In both kinds of case, we are faced with the question "Is claim C true?" (e.g., "Did the butler kill the maid?," "Was the temperature 78?"). In the first kind of case, we have significant evidence *both for and against* C that more or less cancel each other out and we are forced to admit that the *overall* evidence, pro and con, doesn't really point towards C's truth or C's falsehood. We encounter such situations all the time in jury cases when the defense attorney as well as the prosecuting attorney provides strong evidence. In the other kind of case in which we should suspend judgment, we are again faced with the question "Is claim C true?" but we have no good evidence either way: we have no decent evidence for or against C. For instance, faced with the question "Did the planet Venus ever have living bacteria on it?," I haven't the faintest idea what the answer is. I know very little about Venus other than it's about the same size as Earth, it's hotter, it's closer to the Sun, and it's covered in gases. This information tells me next to nothing regarding whether it ever had living bacteria on it. (I could find out a lot more with a few minutes of research, but then I'd ruin the example!) Other people may have excellent evidence either way (e.g., they might be astronomers), but that would just mean that they have evidence that I don't have.

Suspending judgment is often a temporary thing, as this story shows.

18 The Fork in the Road

You are walking through the woods on a path and come to a fork in the road. There are no signs or other indications as to which path goes where. You have to make a decision about what to do. What you would like is to know whether "The right path leads to our destination" is true. (If you knew it was true, you'd pick the right path; if you knew it was false, you'd pick the left path.)

You might reasonably *choose* the left path, but you'd be foolish to *believe* that you have chosen the path that in fact leads to your destination. You simply don't know which path is the correct one, and you have to live with some uncertainty for a while. Only a fool has an opinion as to which path is the true one – even though you will have to make a choice as to what to do. Wisdom often requires us to say "The evidence we have is not good." You are forced to make a choice as to *action* – you have to pick a path – but you are not forced to make a choice as to *belief* – as you can suspend judgment. In that respect, action is very different from belief. Despite all that, eventually you will get evidence as to whether you took the correct path (e.g., after you have followed the path right to your destination); so the suspension of judgment will have been temporary.

Other times the suspension of judgment might never end. For instance, astronomers might start out thinking that Venus could never have had living bacteria on it. But then they discover a way that it might have had bacteria on it but only a billion years ago. So, they suspend judgment. And this suspension might last forever because they are well aware that there is no way to know whether Venus actually had bacteria on it a billion years ago.

Suspending judgment doesn't mean giving up, sitting on your hands, and becoming a bystander watching the world pass by. For instance, a doctor needs to figure out how to treat a specific patient. She can either operate or use medications. She might decide that the two options are equally good, all things considered (cost, pain, etc.). So, if a colleague asked her "Which option is best?," she would have to say that she doesn't know. She has suspended judgment on both "Operating is best in this particular case" and "Medications are best in this particular case." But that doesn't mean she isn't going to do anything. She still has to treat the patient. So, she will probably choose somewhat arbitrarily which option to take. And her choosing (e.g., the meds) doesn't mean that she has made a judgment. She's made a choice on what to *do*, but not on what to *believe*. *Suspending judgment ≠ not acting.* We will look carefully at disagreements over actions in section 9.

So there are many cases of disagreement in which it's not difficult to answer either the Better Position Question or the Disagreement Question. However, part of what makes the topic of disagreement difficult is the fact that, in a great many cases that we truly care about, the answers to the two questions are not at all obvious. We will see this later in the book. Thus, although questions Q1 to Q6 were easy to answer, the Better Position Question and the Disagreement Question are often hard to answer.

4

Expert Testimony and Higher-Order Evidence

As several of our stories have shown, the topic of expert testimony is often key when it comes to thinking about disagreement. So it's worth taking a moment or two to go over some basic points about it.

As you might guess, expert testimony is not terribly different from regular testimony. You can learn things via testimony from people who aren't experts. For instance, I can answer lots of questions about astronomy that a child might ask me even though I'm not an expert in astronomy. Really, I'm just a competent *conduit* from the experts to the child (and, like real conduits, I can transfer only some things successfully). When you want a reliable source of information about a topic, the natural thing to do is ask a genuine expert, whether the topic is astronomy, history, chemistry, botany, or whatever.

However, relying on what appears to be expert testimony often leads to difficulties; I'll go over four of them here.

First, there is the obvious issue of domain specificity: if you know that Sara is an astronomer, then you know that she is an expert on astronomy, but this implies nothing regarding her expertise in other areas. That's pretty obvious: just because she is an expert on things such as stars and galaxies hardly means she will be an expert in Mediterranean history or baseball or economics. However, there are tricky cases as well. For instance, will she be an expert on Einstein's theory of relativity? What about quantum theory? Suppose Kaitlin is an expert in botany: will she be an expert on evolution? If you don't know much about those fields, then you won't know how to answer those questions.

Second, there are political difficulties. For instance, it's pretty obvious whom one should consult when it comes to the scientific status of theories of our solar system, or plate tectonics, or the health–tobacco connection: in each case one should ask the relevant scientists. And yet, for some *culturally sensitive* topics, non-experts can be fooled into not asking the relevant experts. Centuries ago religious people were told by their religious leaders to ignore what the relevant astronomers were saying about the layout of our solar system: the religious leaders insisted that the Earth was at the center while the astronomers said it was the Sun. And just a few decades ago the tobacco companies expended tremendous efforts in trying to hide or distort the scientific consensus that smoking tobacco is unhealthy. Over the last couple decades we have gone through the same old deception, with many oil companies trying to confuse people regarding the massive consensus about the existence, causes, and threat of global warming. No doubt, fifty years from now most people will know that these companies were headed by selfish, greedy liars, just as in the tobacco case, but right now, thanks to the impressive disinformation campaign funded by the oil companies, that knowledge is much less common. So, even if you want to figure out what the genuine experts think, your task can be greatly complicated by deception.

Something similar holds for the theory of evolution: although experts will tell you that the odds that that theory is false are about as good as the odds that the New York Yankees baseball team will have a 150–12 won–lost record next season, people in the USA (especially, compared to almost all other "first-world" countries) are continually deceived about it. For about thirty years now Gallup polls have shown that around 45 percent of people in the USA believe God created humans in the present form in the last 10,000 years or so, and yet much of science's success is utterly dependent on that very claim being completely false: if the claim were true, there's virtually no way that science could be so successful. This case of deception is importantly different from the tobacco and global warming cases: it's not as though a few religious organizations know the truth but are *intentionally* deceiving the public. Instead, by and large what is happening is that there is an unhealthy ideological source of the *unintentional* deception. It's not always obvious to whom one should turn as a legitimate expert, since dishonesty, trickery, and ignorance are real threats.

Third, there are fields for which there is *genuine* difficulty – independently of deception and ignorance – in figuring who, if anyone, is an expert. Who is an expert on God, or morality, or beauty? Or even movies? Over the last forty years or so, Roger Ebert was the most influential movie critic in the USA. But is he a better judge of movie quality than you are? Well, it depends. If we are looking to him to tell us whether we will *enjoy* a movie, then he might be completely unreliable, provided we have very different tastes. In that case, he would not count as an expert. If we are looking to him to be a good judge of the *artistic merit* of a movie, then maybe he is an expert. It will depend on whether there are experts regarding artistic merit! Are there?

That's a hard question, one beyond the scope of this book. Clearly, Roger Ebert knows a lot more than most of us about the artistic genre of movies: its history, its categories, etc. That knowledge might give him the potential to be a better judge of artistic merit than I, since I know little about movies. But I suppose that someone could have all the "factual" knowledge he has and still be almost blind to the humorous and emotional qualities of movies, which would probably make one a poor judge of artistic merit for a new movie.

Analogous remarks hold for moral judgments. It's hardly clear who counts as an expert in morality. Should it be a philosopher, since the subject of morality has been the province of philosophy for well over two thousand years? Or, if morality comes from God, should religious experts be the experts on morality? And how on earth are we to tell who is a religious expert? Just as in the movie case, there are going to be plenty of people who are experts in the sense that they know a great deal about the history, practices, and beliefs of many religions. That's real expertise, no doubt about it. But that's not to say that any of them are experts about God, for instance. It might be the case that God exists but almost all religions are just horribly wrong about God. Alternatively, maybe there is no God, which again would mean that almost all religions are horribly wrong and perhaps only accidentally right about morality.

We will consider the special issues that come up with regard to morality and (especially) religion at various points in this book.

Fourth, experts often disagree with one another on the very topics in which they are experts. One group says B; another says not-B. For instance, some contemporary physicists say that electrons and other particles arise out of the dynamics of tiny strings; others say they don't. Now, this is probably a disagreement that will never bother you, as you don't have any deep convictions regarding the nature of electrons. But take an issue such as theism – the thesis that God really exists. The people who have examined the putative evidence the longest and with the most care are philosophers. The results of their investigation are particularly interesting: on the one hand, among philosophers there are plenty of theists, atheists, and agnostics (the last consists of those who suspend judgment on the thesis that God really exists); but, on the other hand, a clear majority of philosophers are not theists. I don't have any significant polls to appeal to here, but I've been a philosopher for about twenty years and this is my impression, for what it's worth. So, no matter what camp you fall into – theist, atheist, or agnostic – you can congratulate yourself by repeatedly reminding yourself "There are lots of genuine experts who agree with me!!" But are you conveniently going to "forget" that there are plenty of experts who don't agree with you? In other words, are you going to deceive yourself? We will return to the issue of disagreement with large groups of people later in this book.

A final notion, one often tied to expert testimony and that will loom large when it comes to thinking about disagreement, is *higher-order evidence*. Another story illustrates the notion.

19 Holmes and Homer

Suppose Homer knows that Sherlock Holmes has an excellent track record in murder investigations; he knows that Holmes is investigating the murder of the maid; he then hears Holmes announce after a long investigation that he has done as thorough a job as he has ever done and that the butler definitely did it. Homer knows of no special circumstances regarding this announcement (e.g., the butler isn't Holmes's sworn enemy or anything like that).

At that point *Homer acquires excellent evidence E_1* (Holmes's word and superb track record) that there is excellent evidence E_2 (the "detective evidence" Holmes uncovered in his investigation – evidence Homer has yet to hear) that the butler did it. E_1 is "higher-order" evidence: it is evidence that there is evidence for a certain belief. E_2 is the "lower-order" evidence that would be presented in a court of law.

This is not to say that E_1 is perfectly conclusive evidence. Surely it isn't, as Homer knows full well that Holmes is human: he's fallible like the rest of us. What Homer gained when hearing about Holmes was *strong* evidence E_1 that there is strong detective evidence E_2 that the butler is guilty. That is, E_2 is strong detective evidence for "The butler did it" and E_1 is strong testimonial evidence for "There is strong detective evidence for the claim that the butler did it."

I just pointed out that, even if E_1 is strong evidence that there is strong evidence E_2 for a certain belief B, it might turn out that E_1 isn't perfectly conclusive. In addition, even if both E_1 and E_2 are strong evidence, B might be false: maybe the evidence to which Holmes has access looks and really is impressive, but is subtly horribly misleading in the sense that it strongly suggests the butler did it when in fact he didn't do it. Finally, in rare cases, E_2 might not exist at all even though E_1 does! For instance, perhaps this is the one and only time that Sherlock Holmes has "flipped out" and lied about everything: despite what he said to the media, he has no evidence whatsoever that the butler murdered the maid. Even in that case, though, E_1 still exists and is strong albeit misleading evidence for E_2.

The reason higher-order evidence is important for the topic of disagreement has to do with testimony. If you come to believe something on the basis of some body of evidence, and then you learn that a great many intelligent people believe the exact opposite, that testimonial fact – that they are so intelligent and yet disagree with you – is evidence E_1 that you may have missed something in coming to your belief. What the "missing" amounts to isn't clear. It might be that these other folks have some evidence that you don't have. Or, it might be that you all have roughly the same evidence but they have interpreted it differently. Or maybe something else is going on. In any case, E_1 is evidence that you have screwed up in some way in coming to your belief. A primary question we will consider is this: Is E_1 *strong* evidence that you have fouled up?

5
Peers, Inferiors, and Superiors

Knowing some specialized terminology will help you in the remainder of the book. Suppose that, with regard to a certain question "Is claim B true?," Ned significantly surpasses Jed in several Disagreement Factors and Jed doesn't surpass Ned in any Disagreement Factors. Under those circumstances, Ned is the *epistemic superior* of Jed with respect to that question and Jed is the *epistemic inferior* of Ned on that question. If they are roughly equal on all Disagreement Factors, then they are *epistemic peers* on that question. We will revisit these definitions below, but what appears above is good enough for our present purposes.

Notice that it doesn't make much sense to say simply that X is the epistemic superior of Y: you need to specify a topic at the very least. Einstein was your superior when it came to physics and mathematics, but you are his superior when it comes to twenty-first-century popular music (obviously: he died in 1955). I'm probably your superior when it comes to the epistemology of disagreement, but you may well be my superior when it comes to economics, or biology, or lacrosse, or any one of the topics I know next to nothing about and you have studied with some care. Furthermore, someone may be your epistemic superior on the *topics* relevant to the question "Is belief B true?" even though she is not in a better position than you to answer that specific *question*. We will encounter a story with that lesson below (the Baseball History story).

It might look as though, for any topic or question and any two people Pro and Con, Pro has got to be the epistemic superior, inferior, or peer of Con: he has got to be exactly one of them. But that's not so, at least according to the above definitions of "peer," "superior," and "inferior." Pro might surpass Con in several Disagreement Factors while Con surpasses Pro in other Disagreement Factors: a real mixed bag. For instance, Pro might have evidence Con lacks, but maybe Con is a lot smarter than Pro; alternatively, Pro may have had a lot more time than Con to think about the issue, but Con may be so much smarter than Pro that the time advantage doesn't give Pro much of an edge. In such scenarios, Pro and Con don't fit any of the definitions of "superior," "inferior," or "peer" with respect to each other. This is to say that, when you tally up the factors, no one comes out a clear winner.

Thus, when you disagree with person X regarding belief B, it need not be the case that X is your superior, peer, or inferior with respect to the topics relevant to B – again, according to the definitions given above.

But there are alternative definitions of "peer," "superior," and "inferior" that are useful when thinking about the epistemology of disagreement. For instance, I may know that you are my superior when it comes to one Disagreement Factor and that I am your superior on another Disagreement Factor, but I'm confident that the two factors "cancel out" in the sense that we are *just about as likely* to get the right answer to "Is belief B true?" For instance, although you may be generally smarter than I am, perhaps I have thought about the issue under consideration a lot more than you have; so your advantage in intelligence is more or less canceled out by the fact that I have spent much more time on the question at hand. So I think that, despite our differences, we are in roughly equally good epistemic positions to answer the question: we are equally likely to get the right answer (perhaps each of us is about 80 percent likely to get the right answer).

Cases like that motivate alternative definitions of "peer," "superior," and "inferior":

Likelihood Definitions: Suppose you're faced with the question "Is belief B true?" You have your view on the matter: you think B is true. If you are convinced that a certain person is clearly lacking compared to you on many Disagreement Factors when it comes to answering the question "Is B true?," then you'll probably say that you are *more likely* than she is to answer the question correctly. If you are convinced that a certain person definitely surpasses you on many Disagreement Factors when it comes to answering "Is B true?," then you'll probably say that you are *less likely* than she is to answer the question correctly. In general, you can make judgments about how likely someone is compared to you when it comes to answering "Is B true?" correctly. If you think she is more likely (e.g., the odds that she will answer it correctly are 80 percent whereas your odds are just 60 percent), then you think she is your *epistemic superior* on that question; if you think she is less likely, then you think she is your *epistemic inferior* on that question; if you think she is about equally likely, then you think she is your *epistemic peer* on that question.

So we can define "peer," "superior," and "inferior" in the *factor* way, from a couple pages back, or the *likelihood* way, as just articulated. We will have occasion to use both ways as we proceed.

The two definitions of "peer" don't always give the same results. For instance, Einstein was a lot better than I was at math; it's not even close. And yet, when it comes to figuring out 17×4, his advantages don't make any significant difference: I can figure out the answer about as well as he can. So, even if he far surpasses me on some Disagreement Factors, we are about equals when it comes to the likelihood that we will get the right answer (maybe it's about 99.90 percent likely that I'll get the right answer and it's 99.95 percent likely that he'll get the right answer). This is to say that Einstein is my "epistemic superior" when judged by the factor way but not when judged by the likelihood way.

Whether considered in the factor or the likelihood way, someone can be your peer on belief B when she is only *roughly* equal to you with respect to B. If we demand perfect equality for peerhood, then almost no one is going to be your peer on just about any interesting belief that people disagree about (even though it's not hard to come up with uninteresting or idealized cases of peerhood). People differ greatly on the Disagreement Factors when it comes to most disagreements. But even with the "roughly" thrown in, in most real-world cases it's going to be difficult to know or even have a reasonable belief that you are a peer with someone who disagrees with you. You would need to have excellent overall evidence that the two of you are roughly equal on every Disagreement Factor – or that the inequalities just about cancel out – and we rarely have such evidence. In fact, given the diversity of people's histories with respect to beliefs that give rise to disagreement (so, we are not considering beliefs such as "2 + 2 = 4" or "There are lots of trees on Earth," neither of which generate disagreement), it is going to be rare for two people to *be* peers or have *good evidence* that they are peers.

It is often much easier to know that someone is your superior or inferior. For instance, you know that a ten-year-old is your inferior on many topics and questions, and you also know that Einstein was your superior on many topics and questions. Einstein was your superior when it came to questions regarding the beginning of the universe, and your ten-year-old nephew is your inferior when it comes to questions about World War II. But in a great many cases in life one doesn't know one's epistemic position compared to the positions of most of the people one disagrees with. One might be *able* to obtain a lot of that information regarding comparative epistemic position, but quite often one doesn't in fact get it.

It's easy to make a certain kind of mistake in judging peerhood – at least, I suspect it's a mistake and pretty common. Consider the following as an example:

20 Judging Peerhood

Ava is Marco's neighbor. She is friends with him: they talk when they see each other outside their homes doing yard work, when they attend neighborhood and city events, etc. They have had dinners together and even gone to movies with each other and their respective spouses. She knows that he is about as level-headed as she is, his education is comparable to hers, his childhood was similar to hers, his religious and political beliefs aren't terribly different from hers, etc. But he is not a close friend. When discussing an issue with her husband, he asks her, "What do you think Marco would say?" Suppose the issue concerns something of relevance to the people in the neighborhood – perhaps "Is the government going to raise property taxes in our neighborhood next year?" or "Will the mayor of our city win re-election?" or "Is elementary school X better than elementary school Y?"

It may seem that Ava should think that Marco is her epistemic peer on the question at issue. But, really, she has little reason to think that. It's true that she has no reason to think she is either his superior or his inferior. But that lack of knowledge hardly gives her any significant reason to think that they are peers. After all, just consider how easy it is for one of them to be the superior of the other on those three questions. Maybe Marco bumped into a city council member at the local grocery store who said that she was pretty sure that taxes will have to be raised significantly; perhaps Marco is uninformed of local politics even though Ava knows that he is about as informed as she is about national politics, so he doesn't even know who his city's mayor is; and it could easily be true that Marco is familiar with just elementary school X, not Y, while Ava knows a fair amount about both schools. If all of that were true, which of course could easily be the case, Marco is her superior on the taxes question and her inferior on the mayor and schools questions.

Given her knowledge of Marco, Ava may be in a good position to judge that Marco is her equal on *some* Disagreement Factors: that he is roughly as intelligent as she is generally, say, or that he is about no more biased than she is on the topics relevant to the questions under consideration. That's certainly true. But Ava will probably not be in a good position to have any idea on the other Disagreement Factors – in particular, regarding the key factors of *evidence* and *amount of time* spent thinking about the question. So, she should suspend judgment on whether Marco is her peer.

When discussing the epistemology of disagreement, I have witnessed in my students a strong temptation to go from "For all I can tell, going by what I already know about so-and-so and myself, we are equals when it comes to answering the question" to "So, we are probably peers on that question." For many people, *peerhood seems to be the default position to take*. But it seems to me that this is false. Ava can be confident that Marco is her peer only if she can be confident that either (a) she and Marco are about equal on all Disagreement Factors or (b) although she exceeds him in some factors, this is made up by the fact that he exceeds her in others. But in most cases it is going to be really hard to be at all confident about either of those, even if we are somewhat relaxed on how similar they have to be in order to be "equal." Finally, notice that none of this changes much for the likelihood definitions of peerhood.

We should distinguish between "I don't have any *special reason* to think either one of us has any advantage over the other when it comes to figuring out whether B is true," which is often true because we can't point to any Disagreement Factor that clearly differentiates us (e.g., this is true for Ava when she considers herself and Marco), and "I have good evidence that we are peers," which is rarely true unless "peer" is interpreted *very* loosely – in which case the fact that you disagree with such a peer will tell you almost nothing interesting.

Consider an analogy. I'm going to attend a social function at work. I will finally meet the husband of one of my colleagues. I know very little about him other than the fact that he is probably in his forties. I have no evidence that he is taller than I am; neither do I have any evidence that he is shorter than I am (let's assume that I am of an average height for adult males in my part of the world). But, just because I lack evidence for either "He is taller than me" or "He is shorter than me," it would be silly to conclude "We are roughly the same height." Indeed, I have excellent evidence for "He is either taller or shorter than me," as the odds that we are of about the same height are quite small, given the diversity of heights among adult males in the area where I work. The default view to have is "He probably *is not* the same height as me," rather than "He probably *is* about the same height as me." For very similar reasons, the default view to have is "He probably *is not* my peer on belief B," rather than "He probably *is* my peer on belief B"!

Even setting aside that general issue of identifying peers, for many of the disagreements we care most about – regarding morality and religion – there are *additional* difficulties in spotting peers. If Pro is the epistemic superior of Con when it comes to questions about morality or religion, then Pro must surpass Con in some Disagreement Factors while Con doesn't surpass Pro in any factors – or, at the least, Con's surpassing of Pro is outweighed by Pro's surpassing of Con. On many occasions it can be relatively easy to figure out *some* of the comparisons of factors; for instance, it might be easy to determine that Pro has had more time and better circumstances of investigation compared to Con. And it might be straightforward that Pro is generally smarter than Con in terms of intellectual ability. But what counts as *evidence* in these religious and ethical disputes? When it comes to your opinion that such-and-such an action is morally wrong, what is your evidence? It's often quite a bit easier to identify evidence in the case of beliefs that don't have anything to do with religion or morals.

The difficulties aren't limited to identifying peers: it's also going to be difficult to identify inferiors and superiors in the cases of religion and morals. Sure, on occasion it will be easy: the ten-year-old is clearly your inferior when it comes to questions about marital infidelity. But, in a great many of the cases we actually worry about, it won't be easy at all.

For instance, in the case of religion, many believers in God think that they have *experienced* God: they have actually perceived him somehow, and sensed his power, love, forgiveness, or some other characteristic. And these theists will usually say that atheists and agnostics are missing out: if they had experienced what we theists have experienced, then they would be theists too.

On the other hand, atheists will often accuse theists of poor thinking: they consider that all theistic belief is grounded in some combination of wishful thinking, groupthink, testimony that originates in people who don't know what the hell they're talking about, fatally flawed arguments, and other factors excluding perception and impressive scientific or philosophical evidence.

If we wanted to figure out the comparative epistemic positions of Theo the theist and Agnes the atheist, we would need to find out if they had the same evidence and other Disagreement Factors. But how are we going to do *that*? Theo insists that he has key evidence Agnes lacks: the perceptual evidence he got when he experienced God in his own life. So he thinks he is the epistemic superior of Agnes. Agnes insists that Theo is guilty of wishful thinking or outright delusion whereas she is not. So she thinks she is the epistemic superior of Theo. They are going to insist – for completely different reasons – that they differ in important Disagreement Factors. So, in order for us to figure out their comparative epistemic positions with regard to various religious claims, we would have to figure out if Theo really did experience God or if he is guilty of wishful thinking in coming to believe in God. That's going to be awfully difficult in many cases. In short, it's going to be hard to be confident that one knows the comparative epistemic positions of people with regard to religious positions.

We will return to the case of religious disagreement in Part II. What about *ethics* and judgments about peerhood or superiority?

21 Birth Control

Suppose Pro and Con are married and have children. They disagree about whether to give their fifteen-year-old daughter birth control. A couple years ago, when they last discussed the basics of sex and birth control, they told her they would get her birth control when she asked them for it, although the father, Con, also said that he hoped she would wait to have sex until she was around seventeen; the mother, Pro, didn't say anything about that hope. (Never mind whether any of this was the right thing to say!) The daughter now has a steady boyfriend and has requested birth control for the purposes of having sex (and not some other purpose). On the one hand, the parents Pro and Con are very happy: their daughter came *to them* with the request instead of trying to get it herself. And they like her boyfriend as well. So, things are looking pretty good from their perspective. But the daughter is only fifteen, and the parents differ on whether that is too young. The mom, Pro, says it's not too young, while Con, the dad, says it is too young.

Pro, the mom, is generally smarter than Con on tricky real-life matters such as this, although the difference is not huge. As far as they can tell, they have thought about the issue for a comparable, and considerable, amount of time. There is no real difference as far as distractions or other circumstances of reflection are concerned. Naturally, they differ in relevant background knowledge: Pro and Con will remember different aspects of their own childhoods and how their respective parents dealt with these matters. They have about the same knowledge of the facts of birth control and the facts about teenage sex.

Con thinks that, all things considered, it is morally bad to get her the birth control. By "morally bad" we don't mean anything *outrageously* immoral. Con isn't equating giving his daughter birth control with genocide, for goodness sake, but he does think that, given all the facts about his daughter, sex, birth control, and other relevant factors, she should not go on birth control at this point in her life. Pro disagrees: she thinks it's morally okay.

It's not hard for Pro and Con to figure out how they measure up on some Disagreement Factors such as general intelligence, amount of time thinking about the relevant issues, how distracted they were when thinking about it all, etc. But are they equal in evidence? Well, what counts as evidence when it comes to moral judgments such as "It wouldn't be right for our daughter to go on birth control at this time"?

Some pieces of evidence are obvious: knowledge of their daughter's emotional and physical state, knowledge of the maturity of her relationship with her boyfriend, etc. But that is knowledge of just psychological and physical facts. When Con puts all those facts together he comes up with "She should not go on birth control yet," whereas when Pro puts them together she arrives at the opposite view. How can they determine whether one of them is better than the other at these moral judgments, at knowing how to assess morally the relevant psychological and physical facts? Even if it can be done, in practice we will most often not be able to make confident judgments about who is a better moral judge. And that makes judging comparative epistemic position on moral matters difficult.

In Part II we will revisit the notions of peerhood, including the question of when one should revise one's judgment of peerhood upon discovery of disagreement.

6
Some Results

We have established several results so far in Part I:

1   It is often the case that two people appear to disagree, because one says X while the other says not-X, but in fact they do not disagree because they mean different things by their words. That is, while there are many **genuine disagreements**, there also are many **illusory disagreements**. (We used several stories to show this: Abortion's Moral and Legal Status, Led Zeppelin's Influence, Michael Jordan's Height I and II, The Great Actress.)

2   There can be genuine disagreement even when the words we use to express the disagreement are vague and open to differing intelligent interpretations (The Greatest Baseball Player).

3   When it comes to disagreement, all the following *Easier Questions* have "Yes" as the correct answer (in parentheses I include the names of the stories that were used to answer the questions):

a)   Is it ever the case that two reasonable people can come to different yet reasonable answers to a single question? (The Jury)

b)   Is it ever the case that two reasonable people can come to different yet reasonable answers to a single question when they have the same data? (The Chemistry Class)

c)   Is it ever the case that two reasonable people can come to different yet reasonable – in the sense of *not stupid* – answers to a single question when they have the very same evidence, including background knowledge? (Restaurant Bill I)

    d)   Is it ever the case that two reasonable people can come to different yet reasonable – in a sense stronger than that of not being stupid – answers to a single question when they have the very same evidence and relevant background knowledge? (Math Skills)

    e)   Is it ever the case that two reasonable people can come to different yet reasonable – in a sense stronger than that of not being stupid – answers to a single question when they have the very same evidence, relevant background knowledge, and ability? (The Economics Class I)

    f)   Is it ever the case that two reasonable people can come to different yet reasonable – in a sense stronger than that of not being stupid – answers to a single question when they have the very same evidence, relevant background knowledge, and ability, and have worked on the question for a comparable amount of time? (The Economics Class II)

4   We have discovered several (not all) primary **Disagreement Factors** that lead reasonable people to divergent yet reasonable answers to a single question: Data, Evidence, Time, Ability, Background Knowledge, and Circumstances of Investigation.

5   There are three basic cognitive attitudes one can take to a claim: **believe** it, **disbelieve** it, or **suspend judgment** on it. Moreover, one can believe or disbelieve it to different **degrees**, as when one person is extremely confident it's true while another person agrees it's true but isn't as confident as the first person that it's true. Those differing degrees are different **levels of confidence**.

6   Suspension of judgment ≠ adopting the other person's view.

7   In some cases suspension of judgment is temporary; in other cases it is permanent.

8   One key thing to ask about the epistemology of disagreement is the **Disagreement Question** "How should you react to the realization of disagreement?"

9   Another key thing to ask, when trying to answer the Disagreement Question, is the **Better Position Question** "Are you in a better position to judge B than she is?"

10 There are three basic answers to the Disagreement Question, each of which is correct for *some* but not all cases of disagreement:
- "You should stick with your old belief B."
- "You should adopt the other person's belief not-B."
- "You should suspend judgment on whether B is true."

11 Suppose, with regard to a certain topic or question, Ned surpasses Jed in several Disagreement Factors and Jed doesn't surpass Ned in any Disagreement Factors. Under those circumstances Ned is the *epistemic superior* of Jed with respect to that topic or question and Jed is the *epistemic inferior* of Ned on that topic or question. If they are equal on all Disagreement Factors, then they are *epistemic peers* on that topic or question. This has to be relativized to a topic or question, as Ned might be Jed's superior on one topic or question, his peer on another, and his inferior on yet another.

12 Those definitions are *factor* definitions. There are the alternative *likelihood* definitions as well: Ned is your peer/superior/inferior regarding a certain question when he is just as/more/less likely to answer the question truly.

13 Whether two people *are* peers, superiors, or inferiors is one thing; whether they *think* they are peers, superiors, or inferiors is another thing entirely. Someone could think Jones is his peer/superior/inferior and be completely wrong in that judgment.

14 The correct answer to a Disagreement Question depends, at least in part, on the details of how your *epistemic position* compares with that of the other person – the person you're disagreeing with. Although we have yet to come up with any precise, exceptionless rules that determine the right answers, we can offer a couple *rules of thumb*:

Superior Rule: If, before the discovery of disagreement, you thought that a certain person is a genuine expert on the question as to whether belief B is true, you are definitely not an expert, she surpasses you in some Disagreement Factors, and you do not surpass her in any Disagreement Factors – so she is your epistemic superior on the question – then, upon realizing that the two of you disagree, you should adopt her view on B or at least suspend judgment (and she should keep her belief).

Peer Rule: If, before the discovery of disagreement, you thought that a certain person is your epistemic peer on the question as to whether belief B is true – so you admit that you have no advantage over her when it comes to judging B – then, upon realizing that the two of you disagree, you should suspend judgment on B.

7
The Peer Rule and the Superior Rule

Do those two rules of thumb, the Superior Rule and the Peer Rule, have important exceptions? *That is another one of the questions about disagreement that is not so easy to answer.* The Toothache story *almost* shows that the Superior Rule is false in some cases: you know you are no expert on pain or nerve endings, the doctors are, and yet you are justified in sticking with your own view. But in that case, although you are aware that the doctors are smarter than you and have more experience and background knowledge than you, you also know you have a key piece of evidence they lack: the painful sensations in your mouth. So, although they surpass you in *some* Disagreement Factors, you surpass them in *other* Disagreement Factors since your body of evidence is much stronger than theirs (as it contains the key, deciding factor). Thus, although they are your epistemic superiors *when it comes to pain and nerve endings*, they are not your epistemic superiors *when it comes to your present medical condition*, as they are missing out on an absolutely key piece of evidence that you have.

Another story *seems* to put pressure on the Superior Rule.

22   Baseball History

Someone like Barry Bonds, who was one of the greatest baseball players in history (even if he did take illegal drugs), knows a lot more than I do about baseball.

Suppose he knows a lot more than I do when it comes to both the history of baseball in general and the history of the Chicago Cubs baseball team in particular; suppose further that we both know that fact about our comparative knowledge. One day, Bonds and I are talking on the phone. A question comes up: "When was the last time the Chicago Cubs won the World Series?" Neither one of us knows the answer off the top of his head, and we admit this to each other: I don't know it because I know little about the history of the Cubs and Bonds doesn't know it because he just can't remember it exactly, although he knows that it was a little over one hundred years ago. While talking on the phone, each of us consults a website to find the answer. The one I look at says "1906," and so I come to believe the answer is "1906." The one he finds says "1908," and so he comes to believe the answer is "1908." I say to him, "It was 1906," and then he says to me, "The website I checked says it was 1908."

With respect to the topics of baseball, the history of baseball, and the history of the Chicago Cubs, Bonds exceeds me in some Disagreement Factors and I exceed him in none. Thus, it is clear that he is my superior on the relevant topics: baseball, the history of baseball, and the history of the Chicago Cubs team. Just for the sake of having a clean example, we can suppose that I don't exceed him in any Disagreement Factor (so, for instance, I am not more intelligent than he is). But do I have to adopt his view or suspend judgment when I discover the 1906/1908 disagreement?

Hardly – at least not yet. In fact, when he tells me he got "1908," I will probably think that he has just misread his website. After all, "1908" looks a lot like "1906," and I know that I read my website carefully (pretend I'm looking right at the figure on the computer screen while he is talking to me on the phone). So, I will stick with my old belief that the right answer is "1906" – and I will be rational in doing so even though I know perfectly well that he's my superior when it comes to baseball history, even the history of the Cubs.

Now suppose he goes on to tell me that he's checked the website again and he's perfectly certain it says "1908," not "1906." So, I can no longer conclude that he has simply misread the date. Even so, it's arguable that there is no good reason for me to adopt his view, at least not yet. I'm looking right at my website and it clearly says "1906." And I can see perfectly well that it's a legitimate website: perhaps it's ESPN, which is the primary outlet for sports television viewing in the USA. Despite his superiority, I have come across no good reason to trust his website over mine. Since I'm certain that my website is authoritative, I would be quite reasonable in concluding that he must be looking at some computer-generated website that gathers statistics from other sources via flawed computer programs (I know that there are plenty of such websites). I would think to myself: "What the hell is going on? I'm looking right at the statistic from ESPN! ESPN can't be wrong about a basic statistic like this. Bonds must be looking at some garbage website." Those are the reasonable thoughts that might pass through my mind. Until I know which website he is using I may be completely reasonable in concluding that he must be using an unreliable website. So, I don't suspend judgment and I don't adopt his view – and I do all this rationally.

But then he says his website is Baseball-Reference.com, which I know to be as authoritative as ESPN.com. Well, *now* we have reached the stage in the conversation at which I should suspend judgment on what the correct answer is to our baseball question. I have no good reason to think my website is better than his. Even if mine is right and his contains a typo, I don't have any reason to think that's the way things are: it's just as likely that mine had the typo and his is accurate.

This story is a good one because it illustrates a *progression of appropriate responses* that is typical in disagreements. When you first discover that you disagree with someone, it is often the case that you can quite reasonably say to yourself: "I'll bet they just did such-and-such mistake" (as when I thought that Bonds must have merely misread the website). But upon further discussion we often discover that the person we disagree with has made no simple error (as when I learn that Bonds hasn't misread anything and is consulting a website just as authoritative as the one I'm looking at). It can be startling, even shocking, to discover this. When I was a graduate student in physics, at the University of Southern California, I went on a camping trip with some friends of a friend of mine (and, no, it wasn't as awkward as that sounds). They were devout Christians. They asked me what religion I had and I told them "None." Well, that answer just boggled their minds. To their credit, they weren't dismissive of other faiths, but they just couldn't get their heads around the idea of an intelligent person who didn't endorse *any* religious faith at all despite thinking about the issue for many years. A few years later, when I was a beginning graduate student in philosophy, the tables got turned. I was under the impression that *every really good* professional philosopher must think that the central doctrines in Saul Kripke's philosophy book *Naming and Necessity* must be true. I then corresponded a bit with the excellent philosopher Paul Teller, who surprised me by rejecting several of Kripke's theses (he agreed with me that Kripke's book was excellent, but he wasn't prepared to grovel at Kripke's feet like I was). I was naïve!

In any case, the Baseball History story shows that we can discover that we disagree with someone we recognize as our epistemic superior on the topics germane to the disagreement and yet we need not adopt their view or even suspend judgment, at least not initially. One of the keys to that story is that the expert's expertise fails to give him any real advantage in answering *the particular question at issue*.[3] When it came right down to it, Bonds had to do the same thing as me to answer the question "When did the Chicago Cubs last win the World Series?" – consult an authority – and I could do that just as well as he could. Although I knew he had genuine expertise compared to me, I also knew that it didn't provide him with much of an advantage over me in this particular

---

[3] It's true that he had *some* advantage over me: if both of us were forced to guess when the Cubs last won the World Series, without consulting any sources of information, he would have a much better chance of guessing the right answer than I would (as he knows roughly when they last won, whereas I did not). But since he had very little chance of guessing correctly (we can suppose), his advantage isn't significant.

case. And when it became clear that the two "experts" we were consulting – the websites – were divided, then we didn't know what to think, as we also knew that, as far as we could tell, they were equally reliable.

In sum, although Bonds was clearly my superior when it came to the relevant topics, I quickly discovered another expert (the website) that disagreed with him; and then, after he informed me how he was checking his answer – the expert website he was using – I learned that the experts I knew of were in disagreement. And when the experts you know of are sharply divided on an issue, and you know that they know a great deal more than you do on the topics at issue as well as the specific question to which you want the answer, *and* you simply have to rely on them for making up your mind on that question, then it is wise to suspend judgment. The Baseball History story doesn't put pressure on the Superior Rule as much as it shows how the epistemology of disagreement gets complicated by two factors: expertise on a *topic* versus expertise regarding a *specific question*; and disagreement with *multiple* superiors versus a *single* superior. Both factors will loom large later in the book.

The Peer Rule says, roughly, that if you are *convinced* that your epistemic position is the same as that of the person you're disagreeing with – that is, you are convinced that you are epistemic peers – then you should suspend judgment. It does *not* say that if your epistemic position is the same as that of the person you're disagreeing with, then you should suspend judgment. The Peer Rule says that you have actually to *be convinced that the two of you are equal*; it's not enough if you just happen to be equal. To see why the bit about being convinced is necessary, consider another story.

23 Moving in Together I

Jazz and Mark are twenty years old and have been dating for two years. Jazz has come to realize that she and Mark disagree on whether they should move in together. As a matter of brute fact, Jazz knows no more than Mark does about relationships, what it means to combine finances, how to divide up housework and other chores, and the other factors relevant to choosing to move in together. She isn't smarter than he is, she hasn't thought about the issue longer than he has, etc. She is *not* in a better position than he is when it comes to answering the question "Should we move in together?" Even so, it certainly *looks* as though Mark hasn't thought much about the issue. For one thing, he actually *says* that he hasn't thought the issue through properly, whereas they agree that Jazz has done so. When he says this he is being modest, but he gives no outward sign of this. Furthermore, when they discuss the matter, he gets nervous and says things that are not very enlightening, to say the least, whereas Jazz makes many intelligent remarks. In sum, Jazz has every reason to think she knows *a lot* more than Mark about whether they should move in together. But she's wrong: she doesn't know any more than he does about moving in together.

Although Jazz is not in a better position than Mark to answer "Should we move in together?," she has excellent overall reason to think she is in a better position. She has a *justified* false belief that she is in a better position than Mark. But, given that she has excellent overall evidence that she is in a much better position than Mark when it comes to the cohabitation issue, when she discovers that he disagrees with her on that issue, should she say to herself, "Hmm. Maybe I was wrong about that"?

For what it's worth, I think not. If she has *every reason* to think that she's an expert on X and Mark knows very little about X, which is the case here, then it seems to me that she should not react to the realization of disagreement by suspending judgment.

Not only that: if we change the story a little, it seems as though Mark shouldn't suspend judgment either.

24 Moving in Together II

Jazz and Mark are as described in the first half of the previous story. They disagree about whether to move in together and they are epistemic peers on the issue. They have thought of all the same reasons, pro and con, but they weigh them differently. But now imagine that they discuss the issue via email only. Imagine further that Jazz's email to Mark contains only shoddy reasons for her view: she has better reasons, but the document she emails him has only the poor reasons. Same for Mark: the reasons he gives her are not his best ones. In sum, Jazz has every reason to think she knows *a lot* more than Mark about whether they should move in together; and Mark has every reason to think he knows *a lot* more than Jazz about whether they should move in together.

This story illustrates a key point: even if you and the person you disagree with are on a par when it comes to a certain topic – so you are equal when it comes to evidence, ability, background knowledge (including experience), time spent thinking about the relevant issues, etc. – it doesn't automatically mean that *either* of you should suspend judgment when you discover that you disagree with each other. If neither of you has any inkling that you are peers, and each of you has strong evidence that you are clearly superior to the other, then neither of you can be faulted for not suspending judgment. So reference in the Peer Rule to *belief* in equality is a good idea.

In this section we have learned that, when two people disagree about a belief B, at least some of the hard questions about disagreement are the following:

Better Position Question: When you discover that you disagree with someone regarding belief B, do you have good overall reason to think you're in a better position to judge B than she is? (You can also ask this question before you find out she disagrees with you.)

Disagreement Question: How should you react to the realization of disagreement?

Rules Question: Do the Superior Rule and the Peer Rule have exceptions? If so, when are the rules false? And what rules are more accurate?

8
Disagreement over Facts, Values, and Religion

We disagree about straightforward facts just as much as we disagree about values. For instance, we might disagree over "Mark Twain was left-handed" as well as over value questions such as "The US capital punishment system is immoral," "The music group Black Sabbath was better than the other group Metallica," and "Jesus is the Messiah."

Perhaps more important are our disagreements over facts that have a large bearing on our lives. This is obvious from questions such as these, each of which leads to disagreement about facts:

- Is global warming going to be catastrophic if we don't take immediate and significant action?
- Was the 2011 US military action in Libya against US law?
- Will the *Citizens United* legal decision by the US Supreme Court mean US political elections will be dominated even more by people who are extremely rich?

But it's also true that disputes over factual claims are important when it comes to value judgments. Take torture, for instance. In the first decade of the twenty-first century the USA engaged in many "advanced interrogation techniques," including waterboarding. Did this amount to torture, as most scholars thought? Was it unethical?

Those two questions are not the same. On the face of it, the first question is factual and the second question is evaluative: whether what the USA did amounted to torture depends on the factual issue of whether its techniques fit the definition of "torture"; whether those techniques were immoral is a value issue. But the answer to the first, factual, question affects how people *evaluate* those techniques. If it turns out that waterboarding fits the definition of "torture," then waterboarding is torture; and, if waterboarding is torture then, since torture is illegal in the USA, waterboarding is illegal; and, if it is illegal, then people will be strongly inclined to think it's immoral as well. Thus, purely factual questions have profound consequences for our *attitudes* towards moral issues: there is no complete separation of the factual and the evaluative.

Don't fall into the trap of thinking that factual disagreements can always be resolved by looking at our knowledge or evidence. Scientists have often investigated questions that took many centuries to answer successfully. Even the very simple question of why things fall down – "Why is there gravity?" – is still in the process of being answered. The ancient Greeks had an answer, then Isaac Newton did, and then Einstein did, but even today we know that we don't have the full answer, although we are getting closer to it. It may well prove to be beyond our capacity to understand fully.

Religious beliefs are not the same as value judgments. For instance, most Christians think Jesus rose from the dead; that's obviously a religious belief. (Whether or not this is true won't concern us in this book.) But this hardly seems like a subjective matter or a matter of ethics. Either a certain guy, Jesus, rose from the dead around 2,000 years ago or he did not. What people happen to *think* about his life hardly matters to whether he *really did* rise from the dead. Whether or not he rose from the dead is as objective as whether he was left-handed, whether he ever had insomnia, or whether he knew how to wiggle his ears.

The same holds for the prime theistic belief: that God exists. Again, whether people *think* God exists is hardly relevant to whether or not he *really does* exist. Now, if you put a strange interpretation on "God" – for instance, thinking that "God" refers merely to a concept or other idea that gives people meaning in their lives – then whether "God," in that sense, exists obviously is dependent on what people happen to think. But few people think of the word "God" in that way.

I've just argued that religious beliefs are objectively true or objectively false. And yet, people constantly say that religious beliefs are subjective – and it certainly appears as though they are saying something that has a lot of truth to it. The key to resolving this apparent conflict over "subjective" and "objective" is to see that each of the two terms gets used with several meanings. Often when we say that religious views are subjective we mean things such as the following, each of which is a reasonable thing to say (whether each is *true* is another matter):

- The beliefs have no solid, knock-down proof.
- We tend to be tolerant of the beliefs: if you say that there are tigers that roam Canada, people will ask you for evidence; but if you say that Jesus rose from the dead, almost no one will give you a hard time about it.
- Whether or not people accept a certain religious belief depends not so much on the evidence but on what kind of person they are and what kind of life they have lived: what experiences they have had, what culture they come from, etc.
- Many religious beliefs are actually value judgments, such as "Abortion is morally wrong," which are subjective in the sense that whether they are true depends on what people think and do and feel.

None of those ideas is inconsistent with what I wrote above about the objectivity of the truth or falsity of religious claims. I'm suggesting that most religious beliefs are objective *when it comes to truth*; the four bullet points are consistent with that thesis. In other words, my suggestion can be true even if all four bullet points are true too.

There is another point that is crucial to the issue of how we should react to religious disagreement: the distinction between an *epistemically reasonable* reaction and a *socially acceptable* reaction. Religious belief is peculiar in that it is socially acceptable to hold beliefs even when one admits that one has no significant evidence for them. You may be tempted to think that, in one sense, the answer to the Disagreement Question is very easy when it comes to religious disagreement: stick to your old belief, as it is socially acceptable to do so even in the face of profound disagreement. It's perfectly acceptable to believe that Jesus performed miracles, or that an afterlife Heaven really exists, even if there are millions of people who disagree and you have no evidence to present to them other than "My religious tradition says so, especially the books we say are sacred texts."

I agree with the descriptive generalization "It is socially acceptable just to retain one's religious beliefs even if one is aware of millions of people who disagree and one has no convincing evidence to back up those religious beliefs." That's just a claim about how people *react* (with acceptance) to how people *react* (sticking with their old belief) to disagreement (both *react*s are important there!). But, even if that claim is true, it doesn't mean that people are being epistemically reasonable in virtually always sticking to their religious beliefs in the face of disagreement. Consider an analogous case. It's socially acceptable for parents to overrate their children. No one is going to give me a hard time when I claim that my son is extremely nice and smart. Even so, my evidence for that claim is probably pretty lousy. Therefore, just because we don't give people a hard time regarding their religious beliefs doesn't mean that those beliefs are epistemically justified, by which I mean that they are backed up by good overall evidence (of some kind or other; one has to be pretty open-minded about the forms evidence can take).

So, perhaps a great number of our religious beliefs are either objectively true or objectively false despite the fact – if it is a fact – that they are also subjective in ways that don't have to do with truth. But set aside religious claims such as "God exists" and "Jesus rose from the dead" and focus on moral judgments (as in the fourth bullet point above). Are they objectively true or objectively false – or is their truth or falsity a subjective matter?

Here things get really complicated, deserving of a whole book instead of a few paragraphs (and there are a great many such books). For starters, many but not all people will say that whether a moral judgment such as "Third-trimester abortion is morally acceptable in most cases" is true depends on what people think and feel – how instances of abortion affect us, over both the short term and the long term – but it does *not* depend on what people think or feel about the question "Is third-trimester abortion morally acceptable in most cases?" That is, whether or not third-trimester abortion is morally acceptable depends on *objective facts about how it affects us* – just as how whether or not Lady Gaga is famous depends on *objective facts* about what people know about her. Even if almost everyone in the USA in 2013 said "Lady Gaga isn't famous," they could be wrong provided, unbeknownst to them, almost everyone in the USA in 2013 did indeed know about Lady Gaga; to that extent, "Lady Gaga is famous" is perfectly objective, as it can be true regardless of whether we believe it's true. Analogously, even if almost everyone in the USA in 2013 said "Third-trimester abortion is morally acceptable in most cases," they could be wrong provided that, unbeknownst to them, such abortion cases affected us very negatively; to that extent, "Third-trimester abortion is morally unacceptable in most cases" is perfectly objective, as it can be true regardless of whether we believe it's true.

In the previous paragraph I assumed that whether something is morally acceptable depends on how it affects us: whether it makes us happy or helps us flourish or increases our well-being. But many people have thought that whether something is moral depends on what God commands, or on some rules such as the Golden Rule of "treat others as you would want to be treated." I'm not going to say anything regarding who is right about the ultimate nature of morality! However, when it comes to the objectivity of morality, many of these alternative theories say that moral judgments are objective in the same sense as before: whether a specific moral judgment J is true doesn't depend on whether anyone *thinks* J is true or on what evidence people have for or against that judgment J. For instance, if everyone thought doing X was immoral but God had actually made a commandment that we do X (and we had misunderstood his rule or knew nothing about it), then we would all be wrong about what it is moral to do. So, even for that alternative, religious, theory of morality, morality is objective in the sense that it's not up to us at all.

There are still *other* theories about the nature of morality which suggest that whether a moral judgment such as "Third-trimester abortions are morally acceptable in most cases" is true does depend explicitly on whether people think it's true. This is a kind of moral subjectivism. But most people cringe at such theories. They object: "But if that were true, then if a community was severely brainwashed into thinking it's morally okay to torture kids for fun then it would be morally okay to do so in that community!" And then they say that, since it's never morally okay to torture kids for fun, moral subjectivism is false. I won't discuss any moral philosophy in this book, but since moral disagreement is one of the most important kinds of disagreement, we will have opportunities to revisit these considerations later.

9
Disagreement over Beliefs vs. Actions

Recall the Disagreement Question: How should you react to the realization of disagreement? This question is ambiguous: there are several intelligent ways to interpret it. In the next few sections we will tease out the ambiguities and settle on a much more precise phrasing of the question, one that captures what people find worrying about disagreement.

Suppose Jan and Dan are college students who are dating. They disagree about two matters: whether it's harder to get A grades in economics classes or in philosophy classes and whether they should move in together this summer. The first disagreement is over *the truth of a claim*: is the claim (or belief) "It is harder to get As in economics classes compared to philosophy classes" true or not? The second disagreement is over *an action*: should we move in together or not (the action = moving in together)? Call the first kind of disagreement *belief-disagreement*; call the second kind *action-disagreement*.

The latter is very different from the former, as another story will show.

25 Surgery or Medications

Laksha is a doctor faced with a tough decision regarding one of her patients. She needs to figure out whether it's best, all things considered, just to continue with the medications she has been prescribing or stop them and go with surgery. Again, it's a difficult decision, both medically and with regard to the preferences of her patient and his family. She knows it's a tough call. She confers closely with some of her colleagues. Some of them say surgery is the way to go, others say she should continue with medications and see what happens, but no one has a firm opinion: all the doctors agree that, all things considered, it's a close call. Laksha realizes that, as far as anyone can tell, it really is a tie.

In this situation Laksha should probably suspend judgment on each of the two claims "Surgery is the best overall option for this patient" and "Medication is the best overall option for this patient." When asked "Which option is best?," she should suspend judgment.

That's all well and good, but she still has to *do* something. She can't just refuse to treat the patient. Even if she continues to investigate the case for days and days, in effect she has made the decision not to do surgery. She has made a choice even if she dithers (which she won't, as she is a competent doctor). She has to make a choice even though which option she takes will be somewhat arbitrary. Keep in mind, though, that her choice is not *completely* arbitrary. She has done a fantastic amount of careful and expert investigation. If she decides to choose the treatment based on a coin flip – heads means surgery, tails mean medications – this does *not* represent any flippancy on her part, despite the pun.

The point is this: when it comes to *belief-disagreements*, there are *three options* with respect to a specific claim: believe it, disbelieve it, and suspend judgment on it. (And don't forget the more nuanced notion of degrees of belief, mentioned in section 6.) But when it comes to *action-disagreements*, there are just *two options* with respect to an action X: do X, don't do X. Suspending judgment just doesn't exist when it comes to an action. Or, to put it a different way, suspending judgment on whether to do X does exist but is pretty much the same thing as not doing X, since in both cases you don't do X.

Question: when you are deciding what to do about something, are you (a) trying to figure out what you *will in fact* do or (b) trying to figure out what you *should* do, all things considered?

I think it's (b).

26 The Red Onion

It's 4:45pm and it's time for Bryan to make dinner for his family. He's going to make a Greek salad. Unfortunately, when his wife went to the store earlier to buy ingredients she forgot to get the red onion. The onion is pretty important to the salad, but if he went without it the salad would not be ruined. So he's deciding whether to make a quick trip to the grocery store to get a red onion.

I think Bryan is not trying to predict the future: that is, he is not trying to divine what he is *actually* going to do in the next twenty minutes, say. Instead, he's weighing pros and cons and figuring out whether he *should* go to the store. And the "should" here is definitely an all-things-considered "should": two of the things to consider are the facts that making another trip to the store is a pain in the ass and Bryan would rather continue writing his book. So it's not as though culinary considerations are the only ones that count in the deliberation.

One final point on belief-disagreements vs. action-disagreements: often the latter is a lot more important than the former, despite the fact that this book is almost solely about the former. An example:

27   Contested Engagement

You and your partner Chris have just gotten engaged to be married. Isn't that wonderful? Well, it's not for the two sets of parents involved. Both your parents and Chris's parents are very much against the marriage. What make the case interesting are two facts. First, you and Chris acknowledge that both sets of parents are very knowledgeable about what married life involves and how to make it successful. Both sets of parents have been married over twenty-five years and each marriage is quite successful. You and Chris are just twenty years old, and each of you is humble enough to be fully aware that you know very little about marriage – what it's like and how to make it work. The four parents are against the marriage on the grounds that they think the two of you just don't get along well enough to handle married life. Their objection isn't "You are too young" or "You don't have sufficient income" or anything like that. Instead, their objection is that, given your personalities and past experiences, the two of you are going to be at each other's throats in no time. But you and Chris insist that you are entirely devoted to each other, deeply in love, etc.

One could easily think that the *big* question here is not the belief-question "Should you retain your belief that the marriage is a good idea?" but the action-question "Should we go ahead with the marriage?"

Recall the Restaurant Bill I story.

You're at a fancy restaurant with friends and you get the bill, which comes to $215 including the tip. There are five of you at the table and you agree to pay equal shares. You know full well that you and your friend are roughly equally good at doing arithmetic in your heads, without the aid of paper, pen, calculators, etc. But neither of you is very good at it. You both try to figure out how much each person owes, doing the calculation quickly in your heads. You get $43 while your friend gets $45.

When I present this story to students and ask them what the protagonist should do after hearing that her friend got the answer $45 – suspend judgment, stick to her guns, or adopt her friend's belief – I invariably get the response "Why not just do as the friend says? Pay the $45, instead of just $43, and forget about it."

In my opinion, that's the right answer – at least if I was the one at the restaurant. But it's the right answer to a question different from the one I asked them. I asked them what they, in that situation, should *believe* regarding the correct dollar amount. But they gave me an answer to the question of how they should *behave* upon realization of the disagreement. As we have seen in this section, the two questions are entirely different. For my own part, I think the answer to the belief question is "You should suspend judgment on what the share is," but the answer to the behavior question is probably "Pay the amount your friend recommended, $45" (although the details matter for the behavior question, as the extra $2 might not be available for someone at the table). When you're faced with the question "What should you do in that situation?," the use of the word "do" is ambiguous: when I posed that question to my students I meant "What should you believe?," whereas some of my students heard it as "What behavior should you engage in?"

What you do in a situation isn't completely fixed by what you believe should be done. For instance, I may allow my son to do something even though I am pretty sure it's not going to turn out well for him. Perhaps he wants to play tackle football in the basement playroom. Okay, I'll allow it, but I know someone is going to get hurt and end up in tears. This is where the phrase "all things considered" is so important. All things considered, I think it's a good idea that he plays tackle football in the basement playroom. One key factor in the "things considered" is this: respecting his autonomy. Another key factor: giving him the chance to learn something in a vivid way (i.e., that tackling people in a room usually leads to injuries the badness of which outweighs the fun). But if my wife demanded an explanation of why I let them play football in the basement I would not *say* the words "All things considered, I thought it was a good idea." That's because those words tend to get interpreted in such a way that those two factors don't count as "considerations." English is tricky that way. Under the other, more circumspect, interpretation of "all things considered," I do not think that, "all things considered," he should play tackle football in the basement. On that circumspect interpretation I allow him to do something I think should not be done.

How we should behave is a question of *ethics*. There have been many occasions in my life when I discovered that I disagreed with someone, I knew full well that I was right and they were wrong (e.g., I knew that I greatly surpassed them in many Disagreement Factors and they surpassed me in none), and yet I behaved in such a way as to adopt their wishes. The Restaurant Bill I story is an innocuous example, but there are important ones as well. This book is devoted to the epistemology of disagreement, and not so much the ethics of disagreement.

Thus, there are disagreements over *what to believe* and *what to do*. But, despite this distinction, we can achieve some simplicity and uniformity by construing disagreements over what to do as disagreements over what to believe. We do it this way: if we disagree over whether to do action X, we are disagreeing over the truth of the claim "We should do X" (or "I should do X" or "X is the best thing for us to do"; no, these aren't all equivalent). This translation of action-disagreements into claim-disagreements, which I will follow in this book, makes it easy for us to construe *all* disagreements as disagreements about what to believe where the belief may or may not concern an action. Keep in mind, though, that this "translation" doesn't mean that action-disagreements are just like belief-disagreements that don't involve actions: the former still require a choice on what one is actually going to do.

10
What We Should Believe vs. What We Actually Believe

We need to separate two entirely different questions: the question of what we *should* believe/do upon the realization of disagreement and the question of what people *actually* end up believing/doing. The question "What *should* we believe/do upon the realization of disagreement?" is a *normative* question (as it concerns the norms of cognition or action), whereas the question "What do people *actually* believe/do upon the realization of disagreement?" is a *descriptive* question (since it is asking for an accurate description of what people end up doing in cases of disagreement). I would hazard the following descriptive generalizations about how people actually react to the realization of disagreement.

- When a person is faced with a disagreement with someone who is a stranger and who she knows is no expert compared to herself, then generally speaking she will stick with her belief.
- When a person is faced with a purely scientific disagreement with someone whom she knows and likes and whom she knows to be a genuine expert on the matter, then generally speaking she will not retain her belief, assuming that she herself knows that she is not even close to being an expert.
- When a person is faced with a religious disagreement with someone who is a stranger or a friend and who they know is no expert, then generally speaking she will keep her belief.

There is nothing special about these generalizations; I picked three at random that I think are almost always true. Even if these generalizations are true, that doesn't mean that people are *actually* believing or doing what they *should* be believing or doing – in accord with what their evidence says. In this book we are concerned with what we should do upon the realization of disagreement – where the "should" is epistemic, having to do with overall evidence and not with morality. And a central claim of the book is, roughly: if, upon the realization of disagreement regarding belief B, one acquires *new and strong evidence* that one has made an important error of some kind, then one no longer has overall evidence that supports the continued endorsement of B. Recall the Jupiter story: when you read that all astronomers think Jupiter has at least sixteen moons, whereas you learned as a child that it had just twelve, you obtained excellent evidence that Jupiter has at least sixteen moons, not just twelve. It's the addition of the new and powerful evidence that requires you to relinquish your old belief. We will revisit this claim about the connection between new evidence and the realization of disagreement below.

11

Response to Disagreement vs. Subsequent Level of Confidence

We are in the process of making various distinctions that help us make the Disagreement Question more precise. We have discussed beliefs and actions (two sections ago) and norms and descriptions (previous section). We have some more distinctions to work through. When I'm finished with them I'll sum up what we have done and offer the final version of the Disagreement Question.

A person can start out with a belief that is quite irrational, obtain some new relevant evidence concerning that belief, respond to that new evidence in a completely reasonable way, and yet end up with an irrational belief.

28 Totalitarian Japan I

Bub's belief that Japan is a totalitarian state – belief J – is based on a poor reading of the evidence. He believes J despite the poor evidence because he has a raging, irrational bias that rules his views on this topic. Bub has always been firmly biased against the Japanese. His "evidence" regarding Japan is what he reads about it, and what he reads certainly does not suggest that Japan is a totalitarian state! He has let his bias ruin his proper thinking through of his evidence.

> Then he gets some new information: some Japanese police have been caught on film beating government protestors. After hearing this, Bub retains his old confidence level in J.

I take it that, when Bub learns about the police, he has not acquired some new information that should make him think, "Wait a minute; maybe I'm wrong about Japan." He shouldn't lose confidence in his belief J merely because he learned some facts that do not cast any doubt on his belief!

The initial lesson of this story is this: *Bub's action of maintaining his confidence in his belief as a result of his new knowledge is reasonable even though his retained belief itself is unreasonable.* Bub's assessment of the *original* evidence concerning J was irrational, but his reaction to the *new* information was rational; his subsequent belief in J was (still) irrational (because, although the video gives a little support to J, it's not much). The question "Is Bub being rational after he got his new knowledge about the beatings?" has two reasonable interpretations: "Is his retained belief in J rational after his acquisition of the new knowledge?" vs. "Is his response to the new knowledge rational?"

The question "What does rationality demand when one discovers disagreement?" is a *bad* question: it's ambiguous in a way that *matters*. On the one hand, "rationality demands" that, upon his acquisition of new knowledge, Bub drop his belief J that Japan is a totalitarian state: after all, his overall evidence for it is very weak. On the other hand, "rationality demands" that, upon his acquisition of new knowledge, Bub keep his belief J *given that that knowledge gives him no reason to doubt J*. This situation still might strike you as odd. After all, we're saying that Bub is being rational in keeping an irrational belief! But no: that's not what we're saying. The statement "Bub is being rational" is ambiguous: is it saying that Bub's retained belief J is rational or is it saying that Bub's retaining of that belief is irrational? The statement can take on either meaning, and the two meanings end up with different verdicts: the retained belief is irrational but the retaining of the belief is rational. This is complicated, for sure.

This story shows that one's action of retaining one's belief – that intellectual action – can be epistemically fine even though the retained belief is not. By altering the story a bit we can try to show the reverse: how the action can be faulty while the retained belief is fine.

29 Totalitarian Japan II

Suppose that Bub started out with confidence level of roughly 0.95 in J. That means that Bub is about 95 percent certain in the truth of J; he thinks there is about a 95 percent chance J is true. Then he finds out the information about Japanese police beating government protestors. Suppose that the original evidence Bub had justifies a confidence level of only 0.2. (Recall that 0.5 means you give it a 50/50 chance of being true. So 0.2 means you think there is an 80 percent chance J is false and a 20 percent chance it is true.) So, as we said before, Bub has grossly misjudged his evidence. Suppose further that, in reaction to his new knowledge about the police, Bub *did* lower his confidence in J to 0.2 or 0.3 or 0.6 or whatever – whatever level is merited by the correct principles of rationality that make his new position on J rational.

If Bub did lower his confidence in J that way, then *his action of lowering his confidence level would be irrational*. If you have a certain level of confidence in some claim and five minutes goes by in which you correctly and knowingly judge not to have been presented with any new evidence that suggests that your confidence level was too high, then you would be irrational to lower your confidence level – even if you happened to adjust it so that your subsequent belief itself was rational. But that's exactly what has happened to Bub in this second scenario.

Now, if you took some time to reassess your original evidence, then of course you might be justified in changing your confidence level, provided the reassessment went appropriately. But if nothing like that has happened, as in Bub's case, then you would be irrational to change your confidence level. So if Bub did adjust his confidence level to 0.3, say, then, although his subsequent confidence level in J might accurately reflect his total body of evidence – so his position on J would now be rational – his *process* to that rational position would be irrational.

Hence, our two Japan stories suggest two theses:

- If you start with a belief B that's irrational, you get some information relevant to the truth of B, and then you react in such a way as to keep your belief, it can happen that that reaction is rational even though your subsequent belief B is irrational.
- If you start with a belief B that's irrational, you get some information relevant to the truth of B, and then you react in such a way as to come to believe rationally not-B, it can happen that that reaction is irrational even though your subsequent belief in not-B is rational.

And, more importantly, we have to distinguish two questions about the acquisition of new information (which need not have anything at all to do with disagreement):

- After you acquire some new information relevant to a certain belief B you hold, what should your new level of confidence in B be in order for **your new level of confidence regarding B** to be rational?
- After you acquire some new information relevant to a certain belief B you hold, what should your new level of confidence in B be in order for **your response to the new information** to be rational?

The latter question concerns an *intellectual action* (an intellectual response to the acquisition of new information), whereas the former question concerns the *subsequent level of confidence* itself, the new confidence level you end up with, which comes about as a causal result of the intellectual action.

As we have seen with the two theses above, the epistemic reasonableness of the one is partially independent of that of the other.

For my money, the rationality of the intellectual action is the key issue in the realization of disagreement; the question of the rationality of the subsequent confidence level is less important. In brief, when thinking about how we should react to the realization of disagreement, we are wondering how we should *update* our opinions upon gaining that new information. Whether our opinions after the response to disagreement are reasonable depends greatly on whether they started out reasonable. But whether they started out reasonable is an issue *that usually has nothing whatsoever to do with disagreement*. For instance, much recent philosophical discussion can be usefully thought of as centering on the following question:

> Suppose Sara starts out believing B and P, where P is "Nikos is my peer when it comes to judging B." She bases her belief B on evidence E_B and she bases her belief P on evidence E_P. Then she comes to believe D, that Nikos believes not-B; she bases this belief on evidence E_D. Our main question is this: what attitude towards B is supported by her total evidence $E_B + E_P + E_D$?

That's a good philosophical question, but our focus will be on the reasonability of Sara's possible reactions to coming to have D (given that she already has P and B) and not so much whether her subsequent attitude towards B is overall reasonable. We will revisit this point in Part II.

I used an extreme political belief to illustrate the distinction between the rationality of level of confidence and the rationality of intellectual response. There are plenty of important real-life illustrations as well. Pretend that Bub started with a religious belief that had very little or even no backing evidence and was based purely on wishful thinking. When he encounters new supportive evidence for that belief (e.g., he finds out that a really smart person agrees with it), Bub is under no obligation *from the acquisition of that new evidence* to give up his irrational view even though the view is still irrational (finding out that one smart person agrees with you

– when you know that millions don't – does not have the power to make your belief reasonable when it started out based on just wishful thinking).

Or consider this case:

30   The Intruder

Jack hears a bump in the night and irrationally thinks there is an intruder in his house (he has long had three cats and two dogs, so he should know by now that bumps are usually caused by his pets; further, he has been a house owner long enough to know full well that old houses like his make all sorts of odd noises at night, pets or no). Jack has irrational belief B: there is an intruder upstairs or there is an intruder downstairs. Then, after searching upstairs, he learns that there is no intruder upstairs. Clearly, the reasonable thing for him to do is infer that there is an intruder downstairs – that's the perfectly reasonable *cognitive move* to make at this point – despite the fact that the new belief "There is an intruder downstairs" is irrational.

Jack's "cognitive move," upon coming to learn that there is no intruder upstairs, is to infer that there is an intruder downstairs. Bub's "cognitive move," upon learning that the Japanese police beat up some government protestors, is to keep belief J. What we have been seeing is that, in addition to assessing the reasonability of individual beliefs, we can assess the reasonability of cognitive moves.

In Part II, we will look at cases in which this distinction between the reasonability of retained belief and the reasonability of the belief retention will matter.

12
What it Means to Realize Disagreement

Suppose that you think the Japanese attacked Pearl Harbor on December 7th 1941. That's what you seem to remember, although you know perfectly well that you're not a historian, that you're not terribly knowledgeable about World War II, and that this is a vague memory at best. Then your best friend says "Wait. I thought it was December 9th, not the 7th"; suppose further that you know him to be about as intelligent, informed, and careful as you are when it comes to the facts of history. When you learn of his opinion, you will probably become much less confident in your previous assertion. After all, it was a vague memory to begin with. This is a case in which the realization of disagreement has a huge effect – not only *should* it have a huge effect, it actually *does* have that effect for most level-headed people.

But if you believe that Ronald Reagan was a poor president of the USA, and then you find out that this same friend of yours doesn't believe that, well, you are hardly going to be surprised or otherwise affected, right? You *already* knew full well that there are many millions of people with that opinion. Actually bumping into one of them is no great discovery. If you thought that your friend was the world's expert on US presidents and their accomplishments, then you probably would be at least a little concerned that your Reagan belief is mistaken. But if it's clear to you that your friend is not your epistemic superior on this matter, then you will not be troubled. The same holds for millions of highly controversial beliefs. If you think Jesus rose from the dead, or that third-trimester abortion should be legal in all countries, or that baseball is better than basketball, or that there are intelligent aliens in our galaxy, you know that there are oodles of people who disagree with you; so, discovering that Jones disagrees with you on one of those beliefs will hardly be surprising. The *discovery* of disagreement with a particular individual is usually inconsequential when you already knew of the diversity of opinion on the matter.

The lesson: *when you have a certain belief B and you know that there are millions of people who disagree with B, then, when you discover that someone whom you know to be no more expert than you on the matter thinks B is false, you have not been given any good reason to revise your opinion on B.*

This lesson sounds right, but it nevertheless misses the crucial question when it comes to controversial beliefs that you know are controversial: *was it rational to have the controversial belief in the first place, when you first knew how controversial it was?* In this book, when we talk about the "realization" of disagreement, we mean to include cases in which you know there are people who disagree with you even though you may have never met any of them.

13
The Disagreement Question Refined

Let me sum up the most important points of the last few sections. A few sections back I distinguished two kinds of disagreement: concerning a *claim* B vs. concerning an *action* X. I said we are interested in both kinds, and then I explained that a disagreement over the action X can be construed as a disagreement over the claim "We should do X." The upshot is that in this book we are focused on disagreements about claims, which are beliefs. We also saw that we can have three reactions to the realization of belief-disagreement: keep the old belief, suspend judgment, or adopt the other person's belief. We saw that action-disagreements have only two options. Then I distinguished the question of what we *should do* about disagreement from the question of what people *actually do* about disagreement. I said that in this book we are focused on just the former. I tentatively suggested that, when we are concerned about what we're supposed to think when we discover that people disagree with us, what we're really worried about is what the rational *response* is to that realization – not the rationality of the subsequent *belief*, which depends in part on whether we were being reasonable in the first place. Finally, in the previous section I clarified what is involved in "discovering" disagreement.

Combining all those sections, we see that this book concerns the following crucial question, which is our preferred version of the Disagreement Question:

The Disagreement Question, Revised

When you realize that you disagree with someone over belief B, how should you react to that realization in a rational way: retain your belief, suspend judgment, or adopt the other view (keeping in mind that, when it comes to action-disagreements, suspending judgment is not an alternative option)?

Hence, in this book we are investigating what our cognitive reaction should be when we encounter reasons to think we have made errors. You start out believing B and then learn something that appears to suggest that you have made an error (the something in question could be "Jones is wicked smart on this topic and she disagrees with me"). Should you give up your belief in B, or at least reduce your level of confidence in B? That's a rough statement of the Disagreement Question. Clearly, there is no legal or moral prohibition on what we think in response to the realization of disagreement: in that sense, you can believe whatever you want! We have that kind of freedom. But our question concerns what we *should* think, given the evidence and reasons we have. The adult who thinks Hell is located in the center of Earth is free to believe it, but in virtually all cases she should not, since her overall evidence for her belief is pathetic. We are concerned about what you should do – what you should do *in your head*, in your beliefs – in order to be rational.

That's our primary question; there are secondary questions as well. We've already seen some of them. The Better Position Question is "When you discover that you disagree with someone regarding belief B, are you in a better position to judge B than she is?" And then there are questions of whether there are important exceptions to Peer Rule and Superior Rule.

We need to go over three key aspects of the Disagreement Question before we can be confident that we have an adequate understanding of it.

1   When it comes to the Disagreement Question, the notion of rationality is *epistemic*: roughly put, we are concerned with what we should do with our belief *based on the evidence we know about and our prior judgments*.[4] But, even if we have an answer to that question, we may not have an answer to the often more important practical question of what we should do, how we should *behave*, when faced with a case of recognized disagreement. In many cases, as in the Restaurant Bill I story, the practical question of what to do is relatively easy to resolve: just do what makes everyone concerned happy, as there are no difficult moral issues involved. But in many other situations the question of how to behave is incredibly hard to figure out, as it brings up difficult ethical questions.

2   There are "grades of appreciating" the fact that someone disagrees with you. As we have seen, there are easy cases of disagreement – ones in which it's clear that you are completely reasonable in sticking to your guns. The answer to the question for that situation is clearly "Yes." The hard cases occur when you realize that the people who disagree with you are just as smart, informed, honest, unbiased, level-headed, and reflective as you are – or even that they surpass you in those qualities. But there seems to be an important distinction lurking among the hard cases, illustrated as follows. Both Fred and George believe B and know that there are people who disagree with them who are just as smart, informed, honest, unbiased, level-headed, and reflective as they are. Both Fred and George realized this fact at noon on Tuesday. But whereas Fred didn't *do* anything with that thought – he just had it occur to him and then he immediately (e.g., after just three seconds) went on to think about unrelated matters – George spent a great deal of time really thinking it through: "Gosh, these people really are just as smart and informed as I am! I really have no advantage over them at all when it comes to this topic. Why on earth should I think that I'm the one who got things right here?" It's reasonable to think that the pressure on George to revise

---

[4] Even "epistemic rationality" might be ambiguous, as we'll see in Part II.

his belief in B is greater than that of Fred. Fred has *appreciated* the challenge to a much smaller extent compared to George.

Maybe how reasonable it is to stick with your old belief B depends on how deeply you "appreciate" the fact that others disagree with you. We'll look at the hard cases in Part II.

3   When we construe "belief" in one particular way, the Disagreement Question is easy to answer for *all* cases; construed another way, the question is quite hard to answer for many interesting cases. If you construe "belief" in one way, then the answer to the question is clearly "Keep your old belief" *every single time*. But that's not the interesting or troubling way to understand the Disagreement Question. I turn to that matter now.

Here are three basic facts about beliefs:

- Beliefs are true or false.
- Beliefs are expressed by complete declarative sentences.
- You believe something when you accept that it's true.

That's all fine as a partial description of what belief is, but there are a couple of relevant kinds of belief we need to distinguish in order to approach the hard questions about disagreement in a fruitful manner. The difference in the two kinds of belief is tricky.

When you are asked "What is your take on B? Do you think it's true or not?," it seems that, in at least some conversational contexts, especially ones concerning perennially controversial questions, you are being asked to take the main, non-testimonial evidence you know of regarding B and announce how it strikes you as bearing on B. You are not being asked to give your considered judgment on *all* sources of evidence or to take into account what anyone else has concluded – including the relevant experts, if there are any. Instead, you are being asked for something like your *immediate intellectual reaction to that limited body of evidence*. Here's an example.

31 Free Will and Determinism

For many centuries people have debated whether we really have free will. On the one hand, it seems that we have at least partial control over our thoughts and actions. When grocery shopping I can decide to buy Pepsi or not. The choice is up to me, as I'm no puppet: no one has a gun to my head, I don't have any bizarre psychological compulsion that makes me avoid or hoard Pepsi, etc. But then, again, the human body is just another biophysical organism subject to the laws of nature, like any other physical organism. And the laws of nature are deterministic: they say "If a physical object is in such-and-such a physical state and is subject to such-and-such forces, then it *must* move this way." In reality, before I even went to the grocery store, it was determined exactly what physical movements I would execute – including buying the Pepsi. Thus, if determinism is true, then free will doesn't exist.

Jan and Dan are familiar with all that, since they studied it in a philosophy class. When Dan asks Jan, "Well, what do you think? You think we have free will or not?" Jan responds with, "Yes, I do. No one really knows for sure of course, but that's what I believe."

When Jan responds to Dan she is going by *her own* lights, expressing *her own* take on the issue. But did you see the oddity in her response? First she seems to be expressing a definite opinion: we have free will. But in the very next sentence she is saying that no one – including her! – knows whether or not we have free will. If probed further, she would probably say that she was merely "expressing an opinion" to Dan. She is saying that, when she weighs the pros and cons of free will on her own, going by her own lights, she feels as though the pros are winning, even though she ultimately thinks the evidence she knows about doesn't really warrant having any certain view on the matter. When she replies affirmatively she is offering a subjective reaction: "Here is the direction in which I find myself moved when I weigh the evidence myself, ignoring what anyone else has to say on the matter and ignoring the likely fact that I have only a small part of the relevant evidence."

This interpretation of Jan's remarks is bolstered by the fact that many people will be unperturbed that others disagree with them. For instance, if Dan went on to say, "Well, I think free will is an illusion," Jan may well not be bothered. It's not that she thinks there is no truth of the matter. Instead, she thinks (a) that no one really knows, and (b) that, because no one really knows, all we can do is express how the issue strikes us, how we feel about it. So, since feelings are highly personal, there's no problem with Dan feeling one way about free will while Jan feels another way.

I'm not saying that she would be completely okay with Dan's contrary view. She might think that he has pretty much the same evidence she has, and she might think that he's very similar to her in general. So, she might think that he should judge things by his lights pretty much as she does by her lights. That's one reason why she may well argue with him once she hears his opinion.

When I cover the epistemology of disagreement in a classroom, there is always a bunch of intelligent students who immediately think that anyone who has beliefs on extremely controversial matters (such as free will or God) is *way* too confident in her cognitive abilities. Often they are thinking of beliefs in the "overall, considered judgment" sense, not the "inclination, non-testimonial, by my own lights" sense. Other intelligent students are initially completely puzzled as to why disagreement with other people over highly controversial issues should have *any relevance at all* to the epistemic status of their own opinions – even when I tell them that almost every expert in the world disagrees with them regarding those opinions (as the case may be). Usually these students are thinking of beliefs in the "inclination, non-testimonial, by my own lights" sense and not in the "overall, considered judgment" sense. Neither student is making any mistake.

This inclination, non-testimonial notion of belief even shows up in scientific contexts. For instance, I have had plenty of students hear the questions "Was there a beginning to the physical universe?" and "Assuming there was a beginning, did the beginning of the universe have a cause?" in this inclination, non-testimonial manner. (These questions are important when evaluating one of the standard philosophical arguments for the existence of God.) They know that they are in no position to have any real opinion on matters concerning the origin of the universe, as their knowledge of cosmology is almost nil (they aren't arrogant in that way), but when they say things such as "I believe that something caused the universe to start up," they are not being inconsistent because they are merely telling us the view they are *inclined* towards when weighing the considerations they know about, even though they admit that they are no experts and are in no position to have a firm view on the matter. They are intellectually inclined towards a particular answer given a certain base of relevant considerations that bear on the question, but they are humble enough not to "give in" fully to that inclination.

I suspect that people hear the question "Do you think B is true?" in the inclination, non-testimonial, by-my-own-lights manner when two conditions hold:

(i) They are aware of at least some relevant non-testimonial considerations regarding B, so they have some considerations to work with when responding to the question (e.g., unless they are astronomers, they will *not* hear the question "How many moons does Jupiter have?" in this way).

(ii) Either they think the question is highly philosophical or they think the relevant experts (if there are any experts on the topic) have come to no consensus, so they are free to ignore them when thinking about the matter.

In this book we are examining the case when your *considered judgment* (not immediate cognitive inclination) of *all* the relevant considerations (so we include our awareness of what experts think) is that B is true. To take the free will case again, a case of *genuine, problematic disagreement* comes up only when you genuinely fully believe that we have/lack free will and you're aware of someone else who genuinely fully believes the opposite.

14

Disagreement with One vs. Disagreement with Many

Many disagreements are one-on-one: you disagree with a single person and no other person is relevant. In the Moving in Together story, you think the two of you should move in together and then you discover that your partner has the opposite opinion. In the two Economics Class stories, two people disagree with each other. These cases of one-on-one disagreement are profoundly important. For instance, I'm married. Amazingly enough, my wife disagrees with me on many matters. Sometimes the disagreement concerns something trivial, such as what kind of cloth napkins to use for a dinner party. Other times the disagreement is incredibly important. For instance, should we save enough money to send the kids to any university they can get into, no matter how expensive, or should they just go to Fordham University (where I work) for free (so we would send them there regardless of the "fit" issue)? Or should we encourage them to go to universities that aren't outrageously expensive but aren't free either? Final example: my wife and I have a frighteningly annoying neighbor and so we are thinking about moving, which is a huge hassle and costs a fortune. Should we do it?

Cases in which two people need to make an important decision occur constantly; my wife and I have discussed all of those issues in just the last couple weeks. In each of those real-life cases the possibility of disagreement is high and the stakes involved are enormous. Making big decisions is tough; making them when the two of you disagree is even harder. If you are not married and don't have children, you are still faced with comparable tough decisions that will involve your disagreeing with other people, such as your parents, your best friends, your roommates, your boss, your co-workers, or your partner. In each case you are faced with a disagreement with a very small number of people – typically, one or two, sometimes three or four or five (in the case of co-workers or family decisions in which everyone's voice counts).

However, when it comes to many of your beliefs, including some of the most interesting ones, you are fully aware that *millions* of people disagree with you and *millions* of other people agree with you. (We noted this fact a few sections back when we clarified what it meant to "discover" disagreement.) Just consider a belief about religion – just about any belief at all, pro or con. You must have *some* views on controversial matters; virtually every human does. Moreover, you're perfectly aware that they are controversial. It's not as though you believe B, B happens to be controversial, but you had no idea it was controversial. That is going to be true on occasion. For instance, I recall meeting some young children who were stunned to learn that there are people who aren't theists: they had no inkling that theism was controversial. But, for the most part, when you have a controversial belief you know full well it is controversial in the sense that millions of people reject it and millions accept it.

It is easy to feel the pull of the idea that we are irrational to have *any* beliefs that we know to be highly controversial. For instance, perhaps you think third-trimester abortion is immoral. Or, you think it's not immoral. It hardly matters: both beliefs, B and not-B, are highly controversial – and you know that fact provided you haven't been culturally sheltered. Even though you know that there are literally millions of people out there who disagree with you, you continue to insist that they are wrong. Don't try to deny it: if you believe B is true and you also know that millions of people think that B is false, then you are definitely saying that *they are wrong and you are right*. You can't sincerely think that, in *every single case* of apparent disagreement over abortion, the disagreement is illusory!

On occasion, one can be reasonably unperturbed that one's belief is controversial. One thing it depends on is the *community* in which it is controversial. There are innocuous examples of this.

32   Children and Hell

It's controversial among ten-year-olds brought up in fundamentalist Christian communities as to whether Hell is a real place inside Earth. Many of them believe it, many disbelieve it, and many don't know what to think about it.

Needless to say, I think the Hell-is-in-the-center-of-Earth idea is false, and, even though I know that that belief of mine is controversial in certain communities of children and ignorant adults, this provides me with no remotely good reason to alter my view, since it's so clear that I have huge epistemic advantages over them. There are more interesting examples of the same phenomenon.

33   Evolution

It's controversial in certain communities as to whether the theory of evolution is true. For instance, among theists in the USA it is highly controversial, with many people believing it, many disbelieving it, and many not knowing what to think about it.

Despite the facts just listed about the theory's controversial status, I think the theory of evolution is true even though I'm fully aware of its controversial status in those communities. There are several reasons why I am not bothered by the controversy. First, I know that many of the people who dispute evolution have little idea how science works. For instance, I know from experience that scientists almost always withhold judgment on grand theories until the evidence is really impressive; many non-believers don't know this. Second, I know that, in almost all cases in which someone disputes evolution, they are doing so because they are being heavily influenced by irrational religious dogma. This has almost nothing to do with my being committed to atheism: first, I'm *not* an atheist and, second, philosophers know that there is no real conflict between the theory of evolution and the belief that God exists. I'm willing to bet that the theory of evolution contains plenty of errors (depending on what you include in it: the more content it has the more mistakes it will probably have), but in the main it is correct – just like our theories of the atomic nucleus, our theories about cancer, our theories about volcanoes, our theories about elephants, and every other robust scientific theory.

Notice that one could know that evolution is true, and rationally stick with that belief in the face of controversy, *even if one isn't anywhere near to being an expert on evolution.* In fact, that's the way things are with me. I'm certainly no expert on biology or closely related fields. But I do know the absolutely crucial fact: the enormous group of independently minded people best qualified to judge the theory of evolution are virtually unanimous in holding that it's true. So here's another good rule of thumb regarding "highly controversial" beliefs, meaning (roughly) beliefs that are denied by an enormous group of people and affirmed by another enormous group of people:

Controversy Rule: If you have controversial belief B, you become convinced that lots of intelligent people believe not-B (where you believe that some of these people are your peers while others are your superiors or inferiors), but you also come to think that the experts taken as a large group definitely agree with you by a significant majority, then you are reasonable if you retain your belief B.

The evolution example comes from the intersection of science and religion, but there are countless other cases in other fields. In 2011, in some depressingly large political circles in the USA, it was controversial as to whether US President Barack Obama is a socialist, was born outside the USA, and is a Muslim. These ideas were not just false but had no good supporting evidence and enormous amounts of contrary evidence. (We will have occasion to examine political disagreement at the end of the book.) I knew that those claims were false even though they were controversial in some circles and I was no expert on Obama, socialism, or Islam.

By my lights, the most interesting cases of controversy, the ones that give the topic its importance, occur when one doesn't know what the experts think or one knows that the experts are severely divided on the issue. For instance, suppose that you think the death penalty in the USA is immoral – but you know that the experts are severely divided on the issue. Or maybe you have no idea what the experts think but you do know that among the general public the issue is highly controversial. Given either of those situations, you can't comfort yourself with soothing thoughts like "Well, virtually all the experts agree with me, so I can stick with my belief" or "Yeah, I realize people disagree with me, but I'm a total expert on this matter, smarter than almost anyone else when it comes to that topic, so I'm reasonable in keeping my belief."

So, in these interesting cases of controversy, what makes you think that you and others who think like you do have this issue right and those millions of other people are all wrong? Do you really think that your group is their epistemic superior on the issue? Consider what that would mean: you have comparably more intelligence, evidence, reflection, or other crucial factors on that topic.

That's just a set of warm-up reflections; it's not supposed to make you throw up your hands and stop having any controversial beliefs! In Part II we will explore answers to those questions.

15
Some More Results

Let's sum up the main results of the last few sections, continuing the numbering from section 6:

15 We disagree about facts as well as values. Even in science there can be profound, long-lasting disagreements.

16 The Superior Rule and the Peer Rule may well have important counterexamples (the Baseball History story doesn't provide them, but it suggests that counterexamples may exist). We will look at some alleged counterexamples later.

17 Often a disagreement over facts lies "within" a disagreement over values (Torture case).

18 There are disagreements about what we should believe and about what we should do. The latter can be folded into the former as follows: when we disagree about whether we should do X, we are disagreeing about the truth of the belief "We should do X." Disagreements about actions are called action-disagreements while disagreements about beliefs are called belief-disagreements.

19 When it comes to belief-disagreements, there are three options with respect to a specific claim (believe it, disbelieve it, or suspend judgment on it); but when it comes to action-disagreements, there are just two options with respect to an action X (do X or don't do X).

20 The question of what we should believe upon the realization of disagreement is distinct from the question of what people actually end up believing.

21 The question of what we should believe upon the realization of disagreement is distinct from the question of how we should behave upon the realization.

22   We have to distinguish two more questions about disagreement:
- After you discover you disagree with someone regarding your belief B, what should your new level of confidence in B be in order for *your new level of confidence regarding B* to be rational?
- After you discover you disagree with someone regarding your belief B, what should your new level of confidence in B be in order for *your response to the realization of that disagreement* to be rational?

23   The discovery of disagreement is often inconsequential. For instance, when you have a certain belief B and you know full well that there are millions of people who disagree with B, then, when you discover that someone who you know to be no more expert than you on the matter thinks B is false, you have not been given any good reason to revise your opinion on B.

24   Here is the crucial question when it comes to controversial beliefs that you know are controversial: was it rational to have the controversial belief *in the first place*, when you first knew how controversial it was?

25   *The Disagreement Question*: When you realize that you disagree with someone over claim B, how should you react to that realization in a rational way: retain your belief, suspend judgment, or adopt the other view (keeping in mind that, when it comes to action-disagreements, suspending judgment is not an alternative option)?

26   The Disagreement Question is not concerned with belief in the sense of "Here is how I'm inclined to think about the issue, going by my own lights alone." Instead, it's addressing belief in the sense of "Here is my official view on the matter, taking everything into account."

16
Study Questions and Problems

1   There are many little stories in this first part of the book. For each one, list the lessons the story illustrates. This will take a long time, but it will also be enormously beneficial, both in answering the rest of the questions and in mastering the material.

2   List all the Disagreement Factors I listed. Now think of some more factors (if you can). It may turn out that your factors are included as "subsets" of my factors, which is fine.

3   Think of two cases from your own life when you started out thinking that you disagreed with your friend only to discover that the two of you didn't really disagree at all. When you're done with that, say which of the book's stories of illusory disagreement your stories are most similar to, if any.

4   For each of the "easy" questions Q1 to Q6, come up with your own story that shows the answer to the question is "Yes." Or, if you think the right answer to some of the questions is "No," explain why.

5   In typical imaginary or real cases, which do you need to answer first: the Disagreement Question or the Better Position Question? Or does the order change depending on the case? If so, explain why, using some cases.

6   Tell an original story in which it's perfectly obvious that one should suspend judgment upon the realization of disagreement. Tell an original story in which it's perfectly obvious that one should adopt the other person's view upon the discovery of disagreement. Tell an

original story in which it's perfectly obvious that one should stick with one's belief upon the discovery of disagreement.

7   Tell an original story in which Gob and Bob disagree whether belief B is true, where neither is the epistemic superior of the other regarding B, and yet nor are they peers with respect to B – using the factor notion of peers/ superiors/inferiors.

8   On what topics is Einstein your epistemic superior? On what topics are the two of you peers? On what topics are you his superior?

9   Try to come up with your own counterexamples to the Superior Rule, the Controversy Rule, and the Peer Rule.

10   The Baseball History story illustrates how there can be a *progression* of different reasonable responses to the discovery of disagreement. Tell your own story that shows a similar progression.

11   Here is a really bad hypothesis: when you discover that you disagree with someone and you're figuring out how to react to that disagreement, if as a matter of unknown fact your epistemic position is the same as that of the person you're disagreeing with, then you should suspend judgment. Come up with an original story that shows why that hypothesis is *clearly* wrong.

12   Think of a couple cases in which two people are stuck in a disagreement that seems to *combine* disagreement over a belief with disagreement over an action.

13   What is the difference between trying to figure out what you will do from trying to figure out what you should do, all things considered? Or is there no difference?

14   I listed three "descriptive generalizations" that I claimed were true – true for the clear majority of cases. First, come up with some counterexamples to each generalization, thereby showing that they have exceptions. Second, come up with your own descriptive generalization that is true for most cases. Third, come up with one counterexample to your generalization.

15   One can be convinced of something and yet do something else: you are convinced that you/we should do X

but you go ahead and advocate that you/we do Y anyway. Give two original examples of this.

16 Tell your own story in which someone starts with an irrational belief, reacts to the acquisition of new information in a rational way, and yet ends up with an irrational belief.

17 Tell your own story in which someone starts with a completely reasonable belief, reacts to the acquisition of new information in an irrational way, and ends up with an irrational belief.

18 Is the following possible: someone starts with an irrational belief, reacts to the acquisition of new information in an irrational way, but ends up with a rational belief? If so, tell a story that illustrates it; if not, explain why not.

19 Pretend that you think that abortion is morally okay. Your friend Ulrich has always struck you as about as intelligent and level-headed as you are – when it comes to just about any topic worth discussing. Then you find out that he believes abortion is not morally okay. So, you two disagree. Another bit of the story: Ulrich is in your chemistry class and he got a different answer than you did on a really hard test problem. If you're like most people, in the first case the discovery of disagreement won't have much effect on you, psychologically; but in the second case it will. Why is this true?

20 Some people get testy about the topic of disagreement. Here's what the prototypical "angry young man" might say to someone who disagrees with him: "I can believe whatever the hell I want, asshole. No one gets to tell me what to think about anything Goddammit. It's a free country. Who the hell are *you* to tell *me* what to think???" First, point out the truth(s) in his eloquent if colorful speech. Second, explain why, in spite of that deep wisdom, he is not voicing a good answer to the Disagreement Question.

21 I talked about two different kinds of belief: full-fledged and mere inclination. Give your opinion on the matter: (a) Are there really these two kinds of belief? (b) Is the answer to the Disagreement Question different for them?

and (c) Do both kinds of belief play large parts in our lives?

22   Is there such a thing as a *moral expert* – someone who is much better than the rest of us at making true moral judgments? I'm not asking whether there are experts regarding how different cultures think about morality. That's obviously true. And I'm not asking whether some people behave better than others; that's obvious too. I mean: are there people who are experts at figuring out who is *right* about morality (even if they don't always do what they think is right)? For instance, are philosophers who think about morality for decades moral experts in this sense? Or maybe religious leaders are moral experts? Defend your answer. Now answer the same question for aesthetic judgment. For instance, are art critics, or perhaps talented artists, experts at being able to spot great art – better than those of us who aren't art critics or artists?

23   Tell an original story in which Jo believes B, Jo knows that she is no expert on the topics relevant to B, she is fully aware that there is profound disagreement in her country concerning B (with roughly equal percentages of people agreeing with it and disagreeing with it), and yet she is completely reasonable in sticking with her full belief in B.

24   Suppose someone has almost all false beliefs about a certain topic. Could she be a genuine expert on the topic anyway? If not, explain why not; if so, tell a story in which it's true.

25   Tell an original story in which you and Jones realize that the two of you disagree over belief B, you both know that Jones is an expert on the relevant topics while you are not, and yet you both also know that Jones is not in a better epistemic position than you to figure out if B is true.

Part II
Conciliatory or Steadfast?

1
Introduction

Everyone who has thought hard about the Disagreement Question knows that in many ordinary cases one should not keep one's belief. The Jupiter's Moons case was a clear example.

> You think Jupiter has twelve moons. You base this belief on what you dimly recall from elementary school; for a great many years now you have been far removed from science. Then you read in the science section of the *New York Times* that all astronomers hold that Jupiter has at least sixteen moons. You know full well that you're no astronomer, your belief is based on nothing but a dim memory from decades ago during your childhood, and the astronomers are clearly experts compared to you. You're not so arrogant to think that you know more than they do about Jupiter!

However, there are many cases in which a person would be downright foolish to give up her belief just because she found out someone disagrees with her. The Marriage-Slavery story was such a case.

> I remember a student once saying that he thought that being married to someone meant that one is a *slave* to that person. I believe he is wrong. I've been married about twenty years now, I know many couples who have been married for comparable as well as greater lengths of time, and the student in question was nineteen years old and unmarried. Quite frankly, he didn't know what the hell he was talking about, and for all my faults I do know what the hell I'm talking about. I've got tons more evidence and relevant background knowledge than he does when it comes to the marriage-slave

question; and I've thought about marriage a lot more than he has.

We have also looked at some rules of thumb for figuring out whether you should suspend judgment, adopt the other person's view, or retain your belief upon discovering the disagreement.

> **Superior Rule**: If, before the discovery of disagreement, you thought that a certain person is a genuine expert on the question as to whether belief B is true, you are definitely not an expert, she surpasses you in some Disagreement Factors, and you do not surpass her in any Disagreement Factors – so she is your epistemic superior on the question – then, upon realizing that the two of you disagree, you should adopt her view on B or at least suspend judgment (and she should keep her belief).

> **Peer Rule**: If, before the discovery of disagreement, you thought that a certain person is your epistemic peer on the question as to whether belief B is true – so you admit that you have no advantage over her when it comes to judging B – then, upon realizing that the two of you disagree, you should suspend judgment on B.

> **Controversy Rule**: If you have controversial belief B, you become convinced that lots of intelligent people believe not-B (where you believe that some of these people are your peers while others are your superiors or inferiors), but you also come to think that the experts taken as a large group definitely agree with you by a significant majority, then you are reasonable if you retain your belief B.

But there are problems with those rules.

First, there are important exceptions to those rules. We will encounter them below. Second, there are cases of disagreement that those rules don't say anything about. For instance, suppose you know that your belief is controversial but you don't know what the experts think: now the Controversy Rule won't help. Or, suppose you know that the experts are sharply divided on the issue in the sense that 35 percent of them agree with you, 35 percent disagree with you, and 30 percent think there isn't enough evidence to know what to think. Again, the Controversy Rule is silent, even though the thinking behind it suggests that in the 35/35/30 scenario you should *probably* suspend judgment. Or, take a case of one-on-one disagreement in which you were convinced, *before* you learned of the disagreement, that the person in question was your peer. That type of scenario divides into two importantly different kinds: cases in which their answer (which differs from yours) strikes you as reasonable but mistaken, and cases in which their answer strikes you as *clearly* completely mistaken. For instance, given a tough homework question, you will probably be pretty doubtful of your answer if you find out that a recognized peer disagrees with you when she gets an alternative answer that seems pretty reasonable, but, if the question is very easy, you will probably think she just made a mistake this time around. There is a big difference between a case in which the two of you got different answers to a hard problem from calculus and a case in which you say that 17×4 is 68 and she says 17×4 is 218. You should probably suspend judgment in the calculus case but not in the arithmetic case (even before you consult a calculator).

What we would like are rules that we can actually follow in our day-to-day lives. The great philosopher-mathematician-scientist René Descartes once started (but failed to finish) a book entitled *Rules for the Direction of the Mind*; that's what we would like here but applied to real-world disagreement. It's not hard to *start* coming up with an algorithm or decision procedure to figure out what to do, just using the previous rules (see box on p. 110).

I think this is a pretty good if imperfect procedure: if people actually followed it in their lives, society would benefit enormously. But, again, although the advice in the fourth step is good, we need to know whether there are important exceptions. Moreover, in many cases you have no idea at all which group has an advantage or whether they are equal. The decision procedure gives you no advice for that common situation. In addition, it doesn't tell you much about cases in

---

Rough Procedure for Answering the Disagreement Question

First: You find out that someone, or some group, disagrees with you (and your group).

Second: You make sure that this is a case of genuine disagreement rather than a case of people talking past one another on account of linguistic ambiguities and the like.

Third: You try to figure out whether you, or the group of people who agree with you, have a significant overall advantage over the people with whom you disagree when it comes to the Disagreement Factors. So you are trying to answer the Better Position Question applied to the two groups. To do so, think explicitly about the Disagreement Factors as they apply to the two groups.

Fourth: If you have good overall reason to think you or your group has a significant overall advantage, then stick to your guns. If you have good overall reason to think the other group has a significant overall advantage, then adopt their view or at least suspend judgment. If you have good overall reason that the two groups are roughly equal, then suspend judgment.

---

which the disagreement is something other than "We think B is true and they think B is false." For instance, what if you think B is true and your peer, who you know to have the same evidence as you, has suspended judgment on the grounds that she thinks the evidence isn't strong enough to show that B is true? That is a kind of disagreement as well, involving differing levels of confidence in B, and the algorithm above doesn't give any advice about it.

In this part of the book I will present a series of illuminating test cases of disagreement that will help us gain insight into the epistemology of disagreement.

When you realize that you disagree with someone or some group over claim/belief B, there are several categories you can fall into, depending on your thoughts on the Better Position Question:

Category 1: You have never thought at all, even implicitly, about the issue of who is better positioned to judge B correctly.

Category 2: You have thought about it but realize that you have no idea whose position is better.

Category 3: You think you have (or your group has) the overall better epistemic position.

Category 4: You think they have the overall better epistemic position.

Category 5: You think the two positions are about equal.

These categories hold whether the disagreement is one-on-one, one-on-many, many-on-one, or many-on-many (so the "you" and the "they" in the descriptions of the five categories can be either singular or plural). We will hit categories 2, 4, and 5 as we go through the test cases. We will spend most of our time on categories 4 and 5, with a few comments on category 2 in section 7.

When it's reasonable to stick with your old belief, we say that it's reasonable to be *steadfast* in your view; when you have to suspend judgment or adopt the other person's view, we say that one has to be *conciliatory*. So, there are two importantly different ways to be conciliatory.

While most of the ideas in Part I are probably true or *close* to being true – that's why that part was titled "Basics of Disagreement" – I can't say the same for this part! The issues we are about to confront are controversial. *Everything* that appears below – the arguments, the conclusions, and even the issues pursued – is provisional: each is meant merely to spur discussion and thought regarding the epistemology of disagreement. The bitter truth is that it's unlikely that more than a few of the forthcoming arguments are good ones; it's also unlikely that more than a few of the conclusions are true. As I mentioned in the introduction to this book, every time I publish some work on this topic I end up saying things quite different from my previous publications (I suspect that the same is true for others who have worked on the topics for some time). That's not because I'm a fool or a bad philosopher. Rather, it's a reflection of the infancy of the discussion and the difficulty of the topic.

After you have gone through the material in Part II you should be in an excellent position to delve into the more advanced essays on the topic: that's the goal here.

2
Revising the Three Rules of Thumb

We begin by presenting some considerations that suggest the three rules of thumb are probably false even though they are on the right track.

34 Smoking–Cancer

Viktoriya is convinced that B is true, where B is "Smoking causes cancer." If asked, Viktoriya would say, "I am very confident that B is true." Viktoriya is highly confident B is true because she is very well aware that virtually all of the many experts on the topic have long thought that it's true. She has excellent evidence backing up her belief in B. She knows, of course, that there are many people who verbally deny the smoking–cancer connection (e.g., executives of tobacco companies and people desperate to rationalize their smoking habit), but she thinks those people are ignorant, foolish, lying, or caught in self-deception. Viktoriya is also convinced that Willard is her peer on knowing whether B is true. The basis for this belief in peerhood isn't anything fancy or involved: she just supposes that Willard is about as intelligent and scientifically literate as she is, since he is a software engineer like she is and he seems generally knowledgeable about many scientific things in the news (e.g., he knew about the latest mission to Mars). Then she finds out that Willard genuinely thinks smoking doesn't cause cancer.

By my lights, when Viktoriya learns of Willard's opinion she will have acquired little or no reason to give up her belief that smoking causes cancer. When she learned of Willard's opinion she probably thought to herself, "Oh Jeez. He is one of *those* people." She *already* knew about those people; actually running into one won't matter to her overall evidence regarding smoking and cancer. So the Peer Rule looks false.

Peer Rule: If, before the discovery of disagreement, you thought that a certain person is your epistemic peer on the question as to whether belief B is true, then, upon realizing that the two of you disagree, you should suspend judgment on B.

Here is another case that illustrates the same idea.

35   Astrology

Gary is convinced that his fiancé Dave is his peer regarding belief B, the belief that astrology is bullshit. Gary also thinks that the vast majority of experts agree with him. He also thinks that Dave knows about the expert consensus opinion as well. However, he has never discussed astrology or anything like it with Dave; he thinks Dave is his peer on the matter merely because he knows Dave is highly educated generally, just as he is, and he knows that highly educated people almost always know that astrology is nonsense. Unknown to Gary, Dave actually thinks the so-called experts are wrong about astrology. Dave then tells Gary that he thinks astrology is almost entirely right. The subsequent discussion makes it clear to Gary that Dave is being perfectly serious: he really does think that astrology is correct. Gary thinks to himself, "Oh man, he's one of those: he's been brainwashed or something." He drops his belief that Dave is his peer and keeps his belief that astrology is bullshit, with the very same confidence level as before.

This case is tricky compared to the Smoking–Cancer one because the sentence used to express the belief at issue is pretty clearly ambiguous. The trickiness is worth pausing over briefly: in a real-life situation in which it is a clear case of disagreement, what usually happens is that one person is strongly disposed to endorse several disambiguations while the other person is strongly disposed to reject those disambiguations. Regardless, for what it's worth, this strikes me as another peer disagreement case in which one is reasonable in keeping one's initial belief B.

It's easy to get in a certain frame of mind that makes it seem as obvious as anything that one should suspend judgment when one learns of peer disagreement; so the Peer Rule *has got* to be right. After all, in a peer disagreement you *admit* that so-and-so is your peer when it comes to judging B! You just *admitted* that she's just as likely as you are to judge whether B is true; you *agreed that there is no reason to prefer your judgment to hers when it comes to B*; you acknowledged that you have no discernible advantage over her when it comes to judging B. That's what the peer judgment amounts to. Now suppose that the Peer Rule is false and you are reasonable in keeping your belief B. How can that belief retention possibly be reasonable? One second you say you have no advantage over her and there is no reason to think you'll judge B better than she will; the next second you're saying she's got it wrong and you've got it right even though you have nothing like "Well, when she was judging B she got this bit here wrong while I got it right." Nope: you merely heard that she thinks

B is false and, on the basis of that alone, you decided that she must be wrong while you are right. You didn't get to hear her reasons or anything like that; all you learned is that she disagrees with you. There definitely seems to be an inconsistency there in first saying "There is no reason to think I'll judge better than her" and then immediately afterward saying "She judged wrong; I judged it right." What reason could you possibly have for picking "She judged wrong and I judged right" over "She judged right and I judged wrong" when you just admitted that there is no reason?

That defense of the Peer Rule is seductive but I suspect it's wrong. In effect, it's proceeding this way:

> You've already accepted P: the two of you are peers. And now you've discovered that D is true, where D is "We disagree on B." Well, the combination of P and D are good evidence against B. That is, the fact that she is your peer and has judged that B is false is good albeit not rock-solid evidence that B really is false. So, you have now learned of some new and good evidence that B is false. Hence, you should lower your confidence in B at least a bit.

But you could argue this way instead:

> You've already accepted B. And now you've discovered that D is true. Well, the combination of B and D are good evidence against P. That is, the fact that D is true, and that you judged B to be true while she judged it to be false, is good albeit not rock-solid evidence that P is false – she's not your peer. So, you have now learned of some new and good evidence that P is false. Hence, you should lower your confidence in P at least a bit.

Or, for that matter, you could argue this way:

> You've already accepted B. And you've acknowledged that P is true as well: the two of you are peers. Well, the combination of B and P is good evidence against D, the idea that the two of you disagree. That is, the fact that B is true, and that the two of you are peers when it comes to B, is good albeit not rock-solid evidence that D is false – she's

not really disagreeing with you even if it looks like it. So, you have now learned of some new and good evidence that D is false. Hence, you should lower your confidence in D at least a bit.

The fact is, none of P, D, or B is non-negotiable. Perhaps in some cases you should take P and D as relatively fixed and then wonder whether B is false (think of a case when you have conclusive evidence that P is true but only mildly good evidence that B is true). But in other cases – such as the Astrology and Smoking–Cancer ones given above – you should take B and D as relatively fixed and then wonder whether P is true. At the end of this section we will look at cases in which you should take P and B as relatively fixed and give up D, despite appearances.

It's wise to have a variety of examples at hand, so here is another case, a real-world one, which seems to show that the Superior Rule is false.

36 Global Warming

Tessa reads several scientific blogs about global warming, and so has come firmly to believe that global warming is happening. She has read, on many occasions, how the vast majority of climate scientists are convinced that global warming is happening, it is caused mainly by human activity, and its consequences will be staggering. She is going to a dinner party with her partner, and he tells her that his friend's wife Wilma, who will be at the party, is a climate scientist. Tessa implicitly thinks that Wilma must know a great deal more than Tessa does about global warming. At the party she is introduced to Wilma and starts to talk about methods of slowing global warming. Then, much to her surprise, she finds out that Wilma thinks global warming isn't happening at all. Tessa already knew that there were some maverick scientists who disagreed with the consensus of global warming, but she had never met one.

This is an interesting case because it appears to show that there are many situations in which we are aware of dozens of people who disagree with us on the truth-value of B (e.g., Tessa knew this with respect to global warming), we know full well that each of them knows much, much more than we do on the relevant topics, we can see no significant bias or irrationality in their views (no more than we are guilty of), we know full well that each of them is smarter than and just as epistemically conscientious as we are, and yet we are quite reasonable in retaining our own view and thinking that they are all wrong. We see this type of thing all the time in science, as the example illustrates. For instance, 97 percent of scientists with the relevant expertise think B is true; I'm just an amateur who on the basis of their word also thinks B is true; and yet I have always known that there are a few maverick scientists who have the relevant expertise, who display no serious sign of bias or other epistemic deficiency (so these aren't the rare scientists whose opinion has been modified by money), and who are vividly aware that they are in the minority in their disbelief in B (they might think that they are the superiors of the other scientists, in terms of either evidence or ability or some other factor). I stick with my belief in B based on the numbers and percentages of experts. I know that the maverick scientists are my epistemic *superiors* on the relevant topics and question at issue, but I stick with my contrary belief anyway – and I'm reasonable to do so. In Tessa's case B is the real-life claim "Global warming is occurring."

I had Tessa disagreeing with someone she judged to be her epistemic superior on the matter at hand, but the point could easily be made if she thought Wilma was her peer. In any case, the Global Warming story appears to refute the Superior Rule.

Superior Rule: If, before the discovery of disagreement, you thought that a certain person is your epistemic superior on the question as to whether belief B is true, then, upon realizing that the two of you disagree, you should adopt her view on B or at least suspend judgment (and she should stick with her old belief).

You might think that the key to these three examples is in each case the protagonist *already knew* of disagreeing peers or superiors, and the really tricky issue is whether her *first* encounter with disagreement was reasonable. But no: that's not essential to the cases. In each story the protagonist could have started out thinking that "the scientific community" says that B is true (e.g., that smoking causes cancer) but then later learns that really it's just 97 percent of them who do. After learning that latter sociological-epistemic fact she would now be aware of disagreeing peers or superiors *for the first time*, but she would be reasonable in sticking with B because of the extreme percentages involved (97 percent of the experts on B agreeing with her).

One more remark before we leave the Peer Rule and Superior Rule. In the Global Warming, Smoking–Cancer, and Astrology stories, in which I claimed that the protagonist is reasonable to stick with the belief B, I made two assumptions. First, I was assuming that the person in question didn't retain their belief because of something like wishful thinking. For instance, Tessa didn't say to herself, "Well, I'm a lot better looking than Wilma, so screw her." Nor did Tessa stick with B because she was unconsciously turned off by Wilma's odd facial tic. Instead – and this was my second assumption – what was happening was something like Tessa's saying to herself: "I knew there were people like Wilma who aren't ignorant of the issues but who deny B; even so, expert opinion is very clearly in favor of B." The cause of Tessa's belief retention was her sensitivity to the facts about expert opinion, not something that would make her response to Wilma unreasonable. In order to judge whether someone's reaction to disagreement is reasonable, one has to know things other than their opinions and evidence; one needs to know something of the causes of belief retention. Please keep this point in mind when evaluating the stories that follow.

In my opinion, the damage to the two rules is not devastating. Both rules seem to be on the right track; we just need to work harder in figuring out the true principles they are approximating.

One thing we can do in order to find better rules is focus on groups instead of individual people, as the disagreement-with-many cases suggest.

Superior Rule*: If you think that the group you're disagreeing with is in a better position than your group (the group of people who believe B) to judge belief B correctly, then retaining B will be unreasonable.

Peer Rule*: If you think that the two groups are equally positioned to judge belief B correctly, then retaining B will be unreasonable.

In each of the three stories above (Global Warming, Astrology, and Smoking–Cancer) the protagonist knew that her group was in a better epistemic position than the disagreeing group (e.g., in each story she knew that the experts were definitely and quite strongly on her side). And, because she knew this, she was reasonable in sticking with her belief in B. So the above stories don't refute the above revised rules of thumb.

What about the Controversy Rule? Does it need revision too? I think so:

37   Doctors and Doctors

There are 1,000 experts on the topic and the topic is scientific. I know that 75 percent of them agree with me, 15 percent disagree with me, and 10 percent suspend judgment. So far, things look good for me, as I'm aware that the vast majority of experts agree with my view. But then I find out that the *most* expert of the experts, the *very top* experts, all disagree with me. For instance, the belief in question has to do with medicine. The 750 experts who agree with me on belief B are almost all general practitioners (GPs) – the doctors who treat people in ordinary situations, usually outside of hospitals. These people count as experts: they know a fantastic amount of stuff on the topic compared to laypeople. But the 150 who disagree with me are the ones who not only see patients but do a great deal of research relevant to the belief. The problem here is that the findings of the super-experts have yet to trickle down to the GPs.

This story may strike you as a bit unrealistic with all its exact numbers, but the described phenomenon really does happen in medicine and other fields (for instance, the above story is based on a real situation my MD brother-in-law told me about). It even happens in philosophy. For instance, there is a certain view in the philosophy of logic and language called "epistemicism" (it doesn't matter what it is). The majority of philosophers of logic and language think it's false. But the people who are most expert on the relevant topics are much more likely to think it's either true or the view most likely to be true.

I won't offer a fancy revised version of the Controversy Rule, as the revision will end up opaque and too hard to remember. Instead, we can just omit the words "by a large majority," leaving us with this:

> **Controversy Rule***: If you have controversial belief B, you become convinced that lots of intelligent people you respect believe not-B (where you believe that some of these people are your peers while others are your superiors or inferiors), but you also come to think that the experts taken as a large group definitely agree with you, then you are reasonable if you stick with your belief B.

In order to interpret this rule wisely we will have to understand that it's a bit tricky to say that the experts agree with you, as the Doctors and Doctors story illustrated.

Despite our efforts, there is good reason to think the revised rules aren't quite right either: more revision is needed. I'll try to show why next.

I begin with peer disagreement (so this is category 5, not category 4, which has to do with disagreement with folks you believe to be your superiors on B). Our basic situation is the following. You start out with belief B, your first belief. Then you acquire the belief P that so-and-so is your peer when it comes to judging whether B is true or not; that's your second belief. After that, you come to think that she disagrees with you on B: she thinks it's false whereas you think it's true. (The temporal order varies somewhat from case to case, but our set-up captures a good many real-life cases and can be adjusted to fit others.) That's your third belief, belief D (so D is "She disagrees with me about B"). You end up with *three* relevant beliefs, B, P, and D, and our main question is whether you can reasonably stick with B or you have to drop it. As we will see below, in order to answer the question, we will need to pay close attention not only to B but to P and D as well.

Thus, when you hear someone sincerely say, "Well, I think B is false, contrary to your view," you have three claims to juggle: B, P, and D. If you started out confident that both B and P are true but then heard her say that she disagrees with B, you end up faced with a puzzle:

> **The Peer Puzzle**: Given that you think that B is true and that she is your peer, so you think P is true too, you would expect her to judge B in the same way you judged it; but it seems that she didn't judge it the same way as you did, as she said "B is false."

That's the puzzling situation of peer disagreement. So what are you supposed to conclude at this point? There are several possibilities one might consider:

- Does she really not disagree with you, so D is false?
- Or were you wrong about her being your peer, so P is false?
- Or is it the case that she's your peer, B is true just like you thought, the two of you really disagree, and she just happened to foul up when judging B?
- Or were you wrong that B is true?

Those are questions that always apply in peer disagreement cases. Furthermore, by changing the Ps to Ss, we have the questions that apply to superior disagreement cases.

We dropped the Peer Rule in favor of the Peer Rule*. However, there seem to be counterexamples to the Peer Rule*, ones that have nothing to do with experts.

38   Holiday Piano Peer I

Vivianna and Mark are twins who as adults are reminiscing about their childhood – in particular, the times that the extended family got together for holidays. Vivianna has always thought that Mark was about as good as she was at remembering events from childhood, although of course she doesn't have anything like scientific data as proof. She thinks she and Mark are peers when it comes to most claims of the form "When we were kids . . ." She believes this because in the past they seem to have been equally reliable at remembering things. Then Mark says, "I really miss how Uncle Frank played the piano every Christmas. That was such a great thing." Vivianna thinks this is nuts. According to her memory – and it is quite vivid (she can recall detailed visual images of the scenes) – it wasn't Uncle Frank but Aunt Maria who played the piano, it was always Easter and never Christmas, and Aunt Maria divorced Uncle Frank when she and Mark were only about four years old (so for most of their childhood Frank wasn't even around to play the piano even if he happened to know how to play). So, according to Vivianna's vivid memory, Mark has got things completely mixed up: wrong relative and wrong holiday.

Most people would say that Vivianna is within her rights – her *epistemic* rights – to keep her belief B "Uncle Frank did not play the piano every Christmas when we were kids." Thus, it's arguable that the Holiday Piano Peer I case shows that Peer Rule* is false, as the "groups" in question are just the two individuals Vivianna and Mark.

<u>Peer Rule*</u>: If you think that the two groups are equally positioned to judge belief B correctly, then sticking with B will be unreasonable.

Vivianna was indeed convinced that the two "groups" – she and Mark – were equally positioned to judge B, but it wasn't true that she had to suspend judgment on B. We can come up with a disagreement-with-many case that apparently refutes the Peer Rule* as well.

39   Group Projects I

In a college class the students break into two groups
of ten students in order to investigate independently
some complicated matter. Student Stu thinks the groups
are evenly matched, based on his modest knowledge of
their abilities (pretend this is a small college and Stu
knows a great many of his fellow students). After a
week of work representatives of the two groups give
oral progress reports to the whole class. The representative from the other group says that her group has
figured out several things regarding the topic of gay
marriage, including the idea that gay marriage is legal,
in January 2013, in twenty-two US states. But this
strikes Stu as totally off-base. He briefly wonders
whether the student in question is accurately presenting
the verdict of her group, but when he sees the members
of her group nodding their heads he knows that his
group definitely disagrees with their group. Stu is
extremely confident the number is far smaller, as he and
his group members have read many reports on the
issue. He keeps his belief B, "The number of states in
which gay marriage is legal is fewer than twenty-two
in January 2013," and starts to doubt whether the
other group has done much work on the project.

Just as in the other cases, we have a protagonist who starts
with a peer belief P but has much less evidence for it than the
belief the disagreement is about. It's reasonable for him to
keep his belief and reassess P.[5]

[5]You might object: doesn't Stu think his group – the group of people who
accept B, not merely the group of students of which he is a member – is in
a better position than the other group – the group who reject B, which
includes as a subset the other students in his class? It depends how you tell
the story. Stu might not have any opinions about what the experts think.
Or, if you like, you could alter B so that there are no experts beyond the
class members.

The question philosophers have investigated, as is typical throughout philosophy, is *why?* That is, why is it epistemically okay for Vivianna, Gary, Tessa, Stu, and Viktoriya to retain their B beliefs even though in many other cases of peer disagreement (e.g., the Restaurant Bill I and Thermometers stories) it's *not* epistemically reasonable to stick with one's belief?

Of course, there are differences in the stories. In Vivianna's case of the piano-playing relative there are no experts to consult (we can suppose that the relevant relatives have all passed away and there are no photographs or other records to consult). So Vivianna's case is different from Viktoriya's (it's also different from those of the protagonists Gary and Tessa in the Astrology and Global Warming stories). However, I suspect that the factor that secures Vivianna's rationality is the same as the one that does the trick in all the other cases: roughly put, *she has much better overall evidence for B than for P.* That is, although she had a reasonable amount of evidence that Mark was her peer on the matter of piano-playing relatives on holidays, she had much better evidence that Uncle Frank didn't play the piano every Christmas when she and Mark were kids. Analogously, Viktoriya had much more evidence for the belief that smoking causes cancer (that's B) than for the belief that Willard is her peer when it comes to judging whether smoking causes cancer (that's P).

So the crucial factor seems to be the *disparity* between one's overall evidence for B and one's overall evidence for P: when the former vastly outweighs the latter, it's reasonable to keep one's belief B in the face of disagreement. It isn't relevant that one has lots of evidence for B. The crucial factor doesn't appear to be "One has lots of evidence for B" but "One has *much more* evidence for B than for P." By modifying the Holiday Piano Peer I story we can generate an argument that mere extreme evidence for B is not enough to guarantee reasonableness.

40 Holiday Piano Peer II

As before, Vivianna and Mark are twins who as adults are reminiscing about their childhood – in particular, the times that the extended family got together for holidays. Vivianna has always thought that Mark was about as good as she was at remembering events from childhood whether or not they have to do with holidays. Then Mark says, "I really miss how Uncle Frank played the piano every Christmas. That was such a great thing." Exactly as before, Vivianna thinks this is nuts. But in this story Vivianna has incredibly good evidence that Mark is her peer when it comes to recalling events from their childhood – even events involving relatives and holidays. Imagine that they have reminisced a great many times, have tested their powers of recall extensively (using independent sources of evidence, very much like experimental psychologists-detectives), and have come out completely equal in ability to remember accurately the events of their childhood involving relatives.

In this story it doesn't seem as clear that Vivianna is in a position to dismiss Mark's view and keep her belief B – even though she has the very same evidence for B in this story as in the previous story. This time around she finds herself highly confident in *both* B and P; and, by talking to Mark to make sure he really believes what he's saying, she could become highly confident in D ("We genuinely disagree about B") as well (more on that latter claim in a moment). In the first peer disagreement case, Vivianna could reasonably stick to her guns because she had only a mild amount of evidence that Mark was her peer compared to her evidence for her belief B that Uncle Frank didn't play the piano every Christmas when they were kids. But in the second holiday story that vast gap in evidence doesn't exist, and she knows it: she knows her evidence for P is extremely good, just as good as her evidence for B, so she feels torn because she was also highly confident in B.

I like the second piano-holiday story for another reason: *when you are highly confident in both B and P you will feel a lot of pressure to reject D*. In the second story Vivianna will be strongly tempted to think Mark is playing a joke on her! She will think to herself that he just *can't* believe that it was Uncle Frank playing piano on Christmas days, as that is so obviously wrong. She will think that his memory is just too damn good to be so far off – more exactly, his memory is too much like hers to generate such different results. As a result, she will think that he is trying to pull her leg when he seems to reject B: he is just fooling with her. A story by the philosopher Richard Feldman illustrates the same point:

41 The Quad

Suppose that you and I are standing by the window looking out on the quad. We think we have comparable vision and we know each other to be honest. I seem to see what looks to me like a person in a blue coat in the middle of the quad. (Assume that this is not something odd.) I believe that a person with a blue coat is standing in the quad. Meanwhile, you seem to see nothing of the kind there. You think that no one is standing in the middle of the quad. We disagree. In isolation – before we talk to each other – each of us believes reasonably. But suppose we talk about what we see and we reach full disclosure [that is, we have shared our reasons with one another thoroughly]. At that point, we each know that something weird is going on, but we have no idea which of us has the problem. Either I am "seeing things" or you are missing something. I would not be reasonable in thinking that the problem is in your head, nor would you be reasonable in thinking that the problem is in mine.

(Feldman 2006, 223)

Somewhat ironically, I actually disagree at bit with Feldman here. I think the reasonable thing to do in the story he describes is to conclude that the other person isn't being serious, so D must be false. Thus, contrary to Feldman, you need not conclude that there is anything wrong in either person's head. If I look out the window and seem to see as clear as day a person with a blue coat on (and let's assume it's not a case in which the coat is a borderline case of blue or a borderline case of a coat!), and you adamantly disagree with me even after we both take a good long look out the window, I just wouldn't believe that you are really disagreeing with me no matter how much you protested.

I think Feldman is aware of that response. He intended the case to be one in which D is already set in stone. The problem with Feldman's intention is that, when B and P are also set in stone, with vast amounts of evidence backing each claim, it's hard for D to be set in stone as well. That is, if you are completely convinced that both B and P are true, as your overall evidence in each case is outstanding, then you will have a hard time believing D. (We'll look at exceptions to this idea below.) That goes for the Holiday Piano Peer II story as well.

So the Peer Rule* is probably false. Now imagine another variant of the piano story:

42   Holiday Piano Superior

As before, Vivianna and Mark are twins who as adults are reminiscing about their childhood – in particular, the times that the extended family got together for holidays. Mark says, "I really miss how Uncle Frank played the piano every Christmas. That was such a great thing." Exactly as before, Vivianna thinks this is nuts. The thing that separates this case from the others is that, in this episode, Vivianna has *mildly good* evidence that Mark is her *superior* when it comes to recalling events from their childhood – even events involving relatives and holidays. She believes he is her superior on these matters because she has reminisced with him before and she thinks that when they have disagreed in the past he was right a little more often than she was right. She hasn't done any extensive testing of their powers of remembrance, but she thinks he is generally better than she is. She doesn't think Mark has god-like powers of recollection. She thinks he is a *bit* better than her; that's all.

According to her memory, and it is quite vivid (she can recall detailed visual images of the scenes), it wasn't Uncle Frank but Aunt Maria who played the piano, it was always Easter and never Christmas, and Aunt Maria divorced Uncle Frank when she and Mark were only about four years old (so for most of their childhood Frank wasn't even around to play the piano even if he happened to know how to play). So, according to Vivianna's vivid memory, Mark has got things completely mixed up: wrong relative and wrong holiday.

She says, "Are you kidding? How sure are you it was Uncle Frank and Christmas?" Mark replies, "I don't know. It's just what I remember. It's not a really vivid memory though."

So there are three *mild*s here: (1) Vivianna has *mildly* good evidence Mark is her superior; (2) by "superior" she thinks he is only *mildly* better than she is; and (3) Mark says he has a *mildly* good memory that it was Uncle Frank and Christmas (and, hence, a mild amount of confidence that it was Uncle Frank and Christmas). She starts out with belief B ("Uncle Frank did not play the piano every Christmas when we were kids") and belief S ("Mark is my superior when it comes to judging B"). Then she comes to believe D: "We disagree about B." So it's a case of one-on-one disagreement with an epistemic superior.

In my judgment Vivianna is reasonable if she keeps her belief B and just concludes that, despite his superior memory, Mark just got things wrong this time around. She knows he is better than she is *generally*, and he was more likely than she was to judge B correctly, but that doesn't mean that he was guaranteed to judge B correctly if they disagree.

My main point with the Holiday Piano Superior story is this: with the three *mild*s, she is reasonable in retaining B. The main thing that secures her reasonability is her extremely powerful overall evidence for B coupled with her compara- tively mild evidence for Mark's mild superiority and mild belief in not-B.

Now, it's easy to develop the story so that it's *not at all* plain that she can be reasonable in sticking with B: just alter the *mild*s appropriately. If she has overwhelming evidence that Mark is her superior, or she thinks he has god-like powers of recollection, or Mark says his memory of the events is extremely vivid, then it's not clear that Vivianna is reasonable in keeping B. After all, if Mark insisted that his memory that it was Uncle Frank and Christmas was as vivid as any childhood memory, then Vivianna would be in a situ- ation akin to that in Feldman's Quad story: she would know that one of them is really screwed up, and she has no real reason to think it's him rather than her. She would be saying to herself, "Heck, I have long thought he's a little better than me at remembering things like this, but we both have quite vivid yet opposing memories!"

The possible differences in the two ways of filling out the Holiday Piano Superior story are worth pausing over. In my way of filling it out, Vivianna comes to accept two key claims:

- Mark thinks B is false, although he has only a mild amount of confidence because he says he has only a somewhat vague memory against B.
- Mark is generally my superior on things like this, although it's not as though he has supernatural powers compared to me and it's not like I have detailed scien- tific data backing up this judgment about how we compare.

When combined, those thoughts give her some evidence that Mark has *decent but not excellent* evidence against B. In other ways of filling the story out, Vivianna gets evidence that Mark has *extremely strong* evidence against B. Here are a couple of ways of altering the story so that happens:

Way 1:
- Mark is absolutely positive that B is false because he has a very vivid memory against B.
- Mark is generally my superior on things like this, although it's not as though he has supernatural powers compared to me and it's not like I have detailed scientific data backing up this judgment about how we compare.

Way 2:
- Mark thinks B is false, although he has only a mild amount of confidence because he says he has only a somewhat vague memory against B.
- Mark is practically god-like in his abilities to remember things like this even with a vague memory – he is way, way better than I am.

For either of these cases it is hard, at least for me, to figure out what Vivianna should do. This shows that there are two important factors when thinking about the epistemology of disagreement with people one considers one's superiors: the degree of confidence they have in their opposite position on B and the degree to which you think they surpass you in judging B.

Hence, I am *somewhat* inclined to think Holiday Piano Superior refutes the Superior Rule* (although the issues are getting very tricky at this point, so it's unwise to be confident of one's arguments):

Superior Rule*: If you think that the group you're disagreeing with is in a better position than your group (the group of people who believe B) to judge belief B correctly, then sticking with B will be unreasonable.

In the previous stories, the key was that the protagonist's belief in B was much better supported than her belief in P; in this story, B is much better supported than the belief in S, where S is the belief "He is my *superior* in judging B" (where the notion of superiority has to be mild, not extreme).

Don't get the impression that if you're totally, completely confident in B then you get to keep your belief regardless of disagreement. Bad idea:

43 Awareness of Astronomy

Alan is an adult who is absolutely, utterly convinced that the Earth is at rest in space. Alan and his community are pretty sheltered. Then he learns, for the first time, that there are some people who think the Earth is zooming around the Sun. He figures: they must be mentally ill. Then he learns that some of them are actually pretty smart. His response: "Oh well: anyone can be deluded into almost any position, as we're all fallible." Then he learns that all of the enormous number of people who have looked the longest and hardest at the question of the Earth's motion – scientists – are definitely against the Earth-at-rest idea. Then he also learns that these people have used their expertise to do amazing things, such as take trips to the Moon and other places in the heavens.

Even though Alan was 100 percent confident in B, eventually facts about the disagreement can make it unreasonable for him to stick with B. Although that case seems obvious, there are others that you may find troubling.

44 Awareness of Atheism

Theo is absolutely, utterly convinced that God exists – not even a shred of doubt in his mind. Then he learns, for the first time, that there are some people who are atheists. He figures: they must be morons, insincere, or mentally ill. Then he learns that some of them are actually pretty smart. "Oh well: anyone can make a mistake, as we're fallible." Then he learns that an enormous number and percentage of the people who have looked the longest and hardest at the question of whether God exists – philosophers – are definitely on the side of atheism. He also learns that the same holds for the most accomplished of the experts in the hard sciences.

At this point I think Theo is in a position somewhat similar to Alan's. I will have a little to say about religious disagreement later in section 9.

What we have been seeing is that there are situations in which one can be reasonable in retaining one's old belief B in the face of recognized disagreement with people you judged to be your peers or even superiors. But don't you have to reduce your confidence in B *at least a little bit*? When Vivianna learned that Mark disagreed with her she didn't need to give up her belief B, but what if her sister agreed with Mark, and her other brother did as well? Now it's three to one, and the three came to their judgment separately from one another. Surely that makes a difference to whether Vivianna can stick with her belief B!

I think that's right, but it's easy to get carried away here and forget our psychological limitations. Suppose Vivianna started out 95 percent confident in B, in this sense: if we had asked her for a number she would have said, "I'm about 95 percent confident in my judgment." I don't know about you, but I am not sure I'm even *capable* of lowering my confidence "just a tiny bit" – say 5 percent. Lowering your confidence level in a belief is not like turning a dial from "95" to "90." I once had a student who seemed unable to suspend judgment on *anything*: for him, there were just two positions – belief and disbelief – and each was all or nothing (no matter how many situations I gave him in which it's just plain obvious that one should suspend judgment, he would not see the wisdom or even possibility of taking no position; this caused him considerable discomfort). So, even though Vivianna didn't have to suspend judgment after hearing Mark's rejection of B but does need to suspend judgment after hearing that a bunch of independently minded people reject B, this doesn't mean that rationality demands that she make a bunch of little adjustments after each person announces their rejection of B.[6]

So far I have for the most part been arguing that one can occasionally be reasonable in keeping one's old belief B when, roughly put, the overall evidence for B vastly outweighs one's overall evidence for P (in the case of peer disagreement) or S (in the case of disagreeing with superiors). There is another way to get the same results.

In Feldman's Quad case, I start out completely justified in thinking both B and P are true: I can see perfectly well that a person with a blue coat is standing in the quad, and I know full well that you have got as good a view as I have and you're totally healthy and more than able to make the same judgment as I am. So I'm at least 99 percent certain of both B and P. When you start to insist that you don't see anyone at all in or near the quad, blue coat or not, I am reasonable in concluding that you're making a lame joke. I retain both B and P and reject D. We can stipulate that, *as a matter of brute fact*, you have gone temporarily insane and really do disagree with me. So, D is objectively true: this is a *real* case of disagreement. That's fine, but I'm still reasonable in rejecting D

---

[6] Matters might be somewhat different for numerical beliefs. I am going to flip a coin three times and you have to say how confident you are in the claim "At least once you'll get heads." You start out with confidence level 87.5 percent, since for three flips there are eight total possible results (HHH, HHT, HTH, HTT, THH, THT, TTH, TTT), seven have at least one heads, and 7/8 is 87.5 percent. After the first throw, in which the coin comes up tails, you'll adjust your confidence to 75 percent (since there are only four remaining options – THH, THT, TTH, and TTT – and only three of them contain at least one heads). So we can see that, upon acquisition of new information, one can adjust one's confidence level a certain exact amount. (Well, we're idealizing here, as we will know that the coin is not perfectly fair and thus the percentages won't be exactly 87.5 and 75.) And by adjusting the story a bit (make the coin flip ten times instead of three) we can make the adjustment quite small. But I doubt whether this works for non-numerical beliefs in ordinary life.

and keeping B and P, as that's what my (misleading) evidence suggests.

In fact, we can suppose that I am old and have poor but not horrible vision while you are young and have perfect 20/10 vision (pretend that you're an athlete who has discussed his or her amazing vision with me). It's dusk and I know that you are my superior when it comes to vision (although you don't have superhuman vision and it's not as if mine is awful). Even so, despite having eyes that aren't as good as yours, I can see the person in the blue coat very well. In this case P is replaced with S: you are my mild superior when it comes to figuring out if there is a person with a blue coat in the quad.

For the most part, we've been looking at interesting cases in which one can be *reasonable in sticking with B even though one believes P*. By fiddling with the stories we have already looked at, the reader can come up with interesting cases in which one would be *unreasonable in sticking with B even though one believed P*: instead of having the evidence for B vastly exceed the evidence for P (which is what the peer cases in this section have done), have the evidence for P vastly exceed the evidence for B. For instance, the Restaurant Bill I and Thermometers stories both had a protagonist with much better evidence for P than for B, and in each case the reasonable thing to do was suspend judgment on B.

Thus, in this section we have seen two classes of cases of disagreement in which a person appears to be reasonable in sticking to her guns with her old belief B: (1) cases in which her overall evidence for B is much greater than her overall evidence for P/S (but when it comes to the superior case things are tricky, as the three *mild*s proved) and (2) cases in which her overall evidence for (B & P/S) is much greater than her overall evidence for D. With these ideas in mind, we can offer revisions of the rules about peers and superiors:

<u>Peer Rule**</u>: (a) If you believe P, that the two groups are equally positioned to judge belief B correctly, but your evidence for B is much stronger than your evidence for P, then your retaining B will be reasonable. (b) On the other hand, if your evidence for P is stronger than your evidence for B, then retaining B will be unreasonable.

<u>Superior Rule</u> ** : (a) If you believe S, that the group you're disagreeing with is in a better position (but not extremely so) than your group (the group of people who believe B) to judge belief B correctly, but your evidence for B is much stronger than your evidence for S, then your retaining B will be reasonable. (b) On the other hand, if your evidence for S is better than your evidence for B, or your evidence says that they are in a *much* better position to judge B, then retaining B will be unreasonable.

We will re-examine those two rules in the following section.

3
Rethinking Judgments about Peers and Superiors

In most of the stories in the previous section, a person encounters disagreement with someone or some group that she thought was her peer or superior on B, and yet she was reasonable in sticking with B and D. But what happens to her belief in P or S? If she keeps her beliefs B and D, does that mean she should drop her view that the disagreeing person was her peer or superior? After all, she just implicitly said that they got B wrong while she got B right: so how could she still think they are her peers on B?

When the person you disagree with says "I disagree," you have, in almost all cases, thereby acquired good reason to think she believes not-B. At this point, you probably would like to hear her reasons for rejecting B. There are two reasons why you would like to hear her reasons. One, you probably are at least a little interested in hearing if there is any good evidence against B. Two, you are probably wondering how seriously you should take the disagreement. Perhaps you initially thought she was your peer when it comes to judging B. But now that she has rejected B you may want to hear her reasons to see whether she *really is* your peer. If she says things in her defense that indicate that she knows next to nothing on the topics relevant to B, then you'll give up your belief in P. For instance, in the Astrology story, Gary will probably drop his belief that Dave is his peer when it came to judging whether astrology is bullshit. Gary will probably think that the odds are that, if someone thinks astrology is genuine, he or she has had very little training or appreciation of science; since Gary knows that he has a decent training and appreciation, he will conclude that Dave probably doesn't have either. Gary is just going by the odds here: he might not talk to Dave about the issue at all in order to determine whether he is scientifically illiterate. A similar point holds for the Smoking–Cancer story.

But this isn't always true. That is, when you learn that someone thinks not-B, in many cases you have no reason to think P is false. Consider this variant on a previous story:

45   Restaurant Bill II

You're at a fancy restaurant with friends and you get the bill, which comes to $215 including the tip. There are five of you at the table and you all decide to pay equal shares. You know full well that you and your friend are equally good at doing arithmetic in your heads, without the aid of paper, pen, calculators, etc. But neither of you is very good at it. You both try to figure out how much each person owes, doing the calculation quickly in your heads. You get $43 (so belief B is "We each owe $43") while your friend gets $133.

You know, immediately, that your friend made an error. Sure, you knew he was just as good as you at doing this kind of math, and you would have sworn that he was just as likely as you to get the right answer to "How much do each of us owe?" (suppose neither of you is drunk, sleep deprived, distracted, etc.). So, you believed P and B and then discovered that D was true too. You are reasonable in keeping B. But I also think that you are reasonable in retaining P. You would be reasonable in thinking that he just had a temporary *slip*. He just made a little mistake, one that he'll realize as soon as someone points it out (and then you'll all have a good laugh about it). You still think he's your peer on judging B: he isn't drunk or anything like that. He just slipped up on this particular occasion, as we all do from time to time.

For comparison, think of examples from sports. Jack and Jill play the same sport and are peers when it comes to a certain kind of play. On separate occasions Jack and Jill are faced with the exact same play. Even though they are peers, it may well turn out on a particular occasion that Jack handles it well and Jill does not. Jack need not give up his belief that Jill was just as likely as he was to handle that play; given the exact same circumstances he will slip up about as much as she will.

Therefore, in some cases, such as the Astrology one, the reasonable thing to do is give up P while keeping B, but in other cases, such as the Restaurant Bill II story, one should stick with both P and B. So, retaining B doesn't always mean giving up P.

There is another kind of case in which one need not reject P: ones in which a person acquires *more and more evidence for P*. These are particularly important because they can be so surprising when one encounters them in real life.

46 New Software I

Terrance works for a company whose employees have to use complicated software in order to do their jobs. Up until now, the company has purchased the software from several external vendors. This has been inconvenient because the software doesn't really fit the company's needs very well, is difficult to adjust for their particular purposes, and is expensive. So the company has decided to have its computer programmers write some new software that will be designed to do exactly what the company's employees need. Terrance has thought long and hard about this decision and thinks it's a great idea; that's his belief B. Let's say that his evidence for B is quite good. But then he runs into his colleague Telly, who says that he thinks B is false: the new software idea isn't a good one (although he doesn't think it's an *awful* idea). Terrance doesn't know Telly very well, although he would have said, with some but not a great deal of confidence, that he and Telly are roughly peers when it comes to judging the wisdom of the software decision.

At this early point, the reasonable thing for Terrance to do is stick with B and be disposed to suspect that Telly either isn't his peer or has committed a performance error in thinking about the software decision (because his overall evidence for B far surpasses his overall evidence for P). But now here comes the interesting part. Terrance and Telly spend a couple hours going over the pros and cons, and Terrance learns that Telly *knows full well* about all the pros of the decision! It's just that Telly thinks the cons are comparable to the pros. After they discuss the matter at length, Terrance learns that Telly knows all about Terrance's evidence, Terrance knows all about Telly's evidence, but they just add things up differently: Telly thinks the overall body of evidence says that B is false whereas Terrance thinks it says that B is true.

As they discuss matters, Terrance gets more and more evidence for P. Recall that he was initially reasonable in sticking with B in the face of disagreement because his overall evidence for B was much greater than his overall evidence for P. But after discussion that's no longer true, as his evidence for P has gone up a great deal. Does he now have to suspend judgment on B?

Well, there's still the possibility that Telly has just committed a "performance error" as described above. However, that seems a bit unlikely in this particular case, given that Terrance knows that Telly has thought about the issue for many hours over several weeks. Thus, if one's evidence for P becomes really strong and comparable with that for B, one's evidence for D is even stronger, and one realizes that the likelihood of a performance error is very low, then it is *much* harder to see how one can be reasonable in sticking with B. I don't know what to think of Terrance's reasonability in sticking with B in such a situation (and I doubt whether Terrance will know either).

4

More Revision: Confidence Level vs. Evidence Level

Thus far I've focused mainly on cases in which the protagonist has much better *overall evidence* for B than for P: when that happens, it's often the case that the person is reasonable to stick with her belief B after the discovery of disagreement (and a similar point holds when she has belief S, "The person I disagree with is my *superior* on B, albeit not by a huge margin"). That was the basis for the Peer Rule** and the Superior Rule**. However, some relatively simple reflections reveal a wrinkle here, which just goes to show how subtle the epistemology of disagreement topic is.

Despite their merits, I suspect the two revised rules are false in an important way. Consider this story.

47 Ritalin

Roger thinks that it's virtually certain that B is true. Unfortunately, this belief of his is unreasonable because his overall evidence for B is weak. He also thinks P is true, where P is "Sari is my peer on B," but he believes it to a much smaller degree than he believes B. For instance, suppose Roger is a doctor who is interested in finding out why Ritalin helps people with ADD (Attention Deficit Disorder) concentrate longer and better than they would without the drug. He thinks it works because it has characteristic X. Although he has some evidence that X is the reason Ritalin works, it's not very good (for one thing, the evidence he has suggests that the reason Ritalin works is *either* X, Y, or Z, he knows this fact about the evidence, and he has no decent evidence that X is more likely than Y or Z). Despite all that, Roger is 99 percent sure that X is the key; so he has clearly misjudged the strength of the evidence. There are many other doctors who are just as smart and thorough as Roger in their investigations of Ritalin; Sari is one such doctor. Roger has known her for a while, but not for terribly long, and he thinks that the two of them are about on a par when it comes to knowing about Ritalin. But he is only 70 percent sure she is his peer on the matter. This is not because he is arrogant, secretly thinking that maybe he is smarter than she is. Instead, it is quite difficult to make judgments of peerhood on complicated matters, and he is wise to be not terribly confident that she is his peer on this issue. When he discovers that Sari thinks X is probably not the reason Ritalin works, he weighs his confidence levels in B and P – 99 percent for B, 70 percent for P – and sticks with B.

By my lights, Roger is reasonable in sticking with B after the discovery of disagreement with Sari. To be sure, he is being unreasonable to an extent: he was not being reasonable in thinking the evidence for B was excellent. But that's a *prior* mistake – a mistake he made *before* the discovery of disagreement. But because he is 99 percent sure B is true while he is just 70 percent sure P is true, the reasonable thing for him to do – in the sense of his cognitive response to the new knowledge that D is true – is to retain B. We saw the same general pattern when we considered the two Japan stories in Part I: a person can start out with an irrational belief, react to some new evidence in a reasonable way, and end up with an irrational belief. In the Japan case the new evidence was "Japanese police beat up some governmental protestors"; in the Ritalin case the new evidence was "Sari disagrees with me about B." We also encountered the pattern in the Intruder story from Part I. This type of thing happens all the time.

Finally, notice that all this could be true even if Roger thinks that Sari is his *superior* on B. If Roger is 99 percent certain of B's truth, only 70 percent certain of Sari's superiority, and thinks she is only mildly superior to him, then it seems to me that he would be reasonable in thinking that Sari must have made a mistake this time around, as unlikely as that is. Even then, though, his reasonability decreases in proportion to the extent he thinks she is his superior on B: if he thinks she is virtually omniscient when it comes to Ritalin, and not merely a little more likely than him to judge B correctly, then it seems he should be more worried that he has made an error in judging B.

Therefore, Roger's reaction to Sari's disagreement is reasonable even though his *overall* dealings with B – especially what he did *before* the discovery of the disagreement – are unreasonable.

That was a disagreement-with-one case. We can see the same lesson in a disagreement-with-many case by tweaking the Group Projects I story.

48   Group Projects II

Just as in the first group projects story, in a college class the students break into two groups of ten students in order to investigate independently some complicated matter. Student Stu thinks the groups are evenly matched, based on his modest knowledge of their abilities (pretend this is a small college and Stu knows a great many of his fellow students). But he is only about 70 percent sure of this. After a week of work the two groups have representatives give oral progress reports to the whole class. The representative from the other group says that her group has figured out several things, including that gay people can legally get married, in January 2013, in twenty-two US states. But this strikes Stu as wildly inaccurate: he is 99 percent sure that they are wrong. He briefly wonders whether the student in question is accurately presenting the verdict of her group, but when he sees the members of her group nodding their heads at the representative's assertion he knows that his group definitely disagrees with their group. The problem here is that his evidence for his belief B "Gay people cannot legally get married in January 2013, in twenty-two US states" is actually lousy: he has just a dim memory of reading somewhere that the number is five, he knows he can't remember where he read it, and he read that number in just one place – the comments to a blog post, which are famously unreliable, to say the least. He keeps his belief B and starts to doubt whether the other group has done much work on the project.

What is doing the work here is that Stu is significantly overconfident in B: he is 99 percent confident in it even though his evidence is very weak. The Ritalin and Group Projects II stories have the protagonist *reasonably* sticking with B even though the evidence they have for B was *inferior* to the evidence they had for P (or S); the key to reasonability was that the person was overconfident in B (and we could have arranged it so that he judged the evidence for B correctly but was lacking confidence in P or S; it would be valuable for you to try and come up with such a story yourself). Thus, we have argued against part (b) of both revised rules:

<u>Peer Rule**</u>: (a) If you believe P, that the two groups are equally positioned to judge belief B correctly, but your evidence for B is much stronger than your evidence for P, then your retaining B will be reasonable. (b) On the other hand, if your evidence for P is stronger than your evidence for B, then retaining B will be unreasonable.

<u>Superior Rule</u>**: (a) If you believe S, that the group you're disagreeing with is in a better position (but not extremely so) than your group (the group of people who believe B) to judge belief B correctly, but your evidence for B is much stronger than your evidence for S, then your retaining B will be reasonable. (b) On the other hand, if your evidence for S is better than your evidence for B, or your evidence says that they are in a *much* better position to judge B, then retaining B will be unreasonable.

It doesn't take much creativity to see how to flip matters around to argue against part (a) of each rule: that is, we can show that one can be *unreasonable* in retaining B even though the evidence for B is *superior* to the evidence for P or S. We pull it off by having the protagonist considerably overconfident in P or S (or quite lacking confidence in B).

49 New Software II

Just as in the first software story, Terrance's company has decided to have its computer programmers write some new software that will be designed to do exactly what the company's employees need. Terrance has thought long and hard about this decision and thinks it's a great idea; that's his belief B. Let's say that his evidence for B is very good. However, he is only about 70 percent confident in B's truth; so he has misjudged the strength of his evidence. Then he runs into his colleague Telly, who says that he thinks B is false: the new software idea isn't a good one (although he doesn't think it's an *awful* idea). Although Terrance doesn't know Telly very well, when he learns of Telly's view, he is *shaken*. For some odd reason, he is completely, utterly convinced that Telly is his exact peer on this issue: he is totally convinced, without any discussion with Telly, that he and Telly are exactly equally likely to have reached the right decision on B. He has little evidence for this peerhood claim P, but he believes it with absolute certainty anyway.

In this story it is hardly clear that Terrance would be reasonable to stick with B, as the Peer Rule** part (a) dictates. It's arguable that he would not be reasonable to stick with B, despite the fact that his evidence for B far exceeds his evidence for P. And if we alter the story just a bit – make Terrance irrationally convinced of S, where S is "Telly is definitely my superior on these matters" – we can see how Terrance would be unreasonable to stick with B even though his evidence for B is far superior to his evidence for S.

Thus, we have arrived at improved if not exceptionless rules:

> **Peer Rule***: (a) If you believe P, that the two groups are equally positioned to judge belief B correctly, and you are much more confident in B than in P, then retaining B will be reasonable. (b) On the other hand, if you are much more confident in P than in B, then sticking with B will be unreasonable.

> **Superior Rule***: (a) If you believe S, that the group you're disagreeing with is in a better position (but not extremely so) than your group (the group of people who believe B) to judge belief B correctly, but you are much more confident in B than in S, then your retaining B will be reasonable. (b) On the other hand, if you are much more confident in S than in B, or your S belief says that they are in a *much* better position to judge B, then sticking with B will be unreasonable.

Philosophers are good at formulating plausible philosophical principles and then finding strange counterexamples to those theories. In this book I bring up counterexamples only when I think they matter to real-life disagreements. I suspect that there are counterexamples to these *** rules as well, although they are getting further and further from ordinary life. Here we go:

The Restaurant Bill II story suggests that part (b) of the Peer Rule*** is false. In that story we can imagine that you are very confident in P: you have done many math exercises with your friend and have compared track records in detail. The comparison has convinced you that neither of you is a genius at doing calculations in your head, but it has also shown that neither of you is bad at it either. When she gets $133 for an answer, you can safely assume that she has just slipped up this time, as discussed above. You are reasonable in sticking with B ("We each owe $43") even though your confidence in P ("We are peers on B") is stronger than your confidence in B. You are reasonable because you have acquired some information – her answer to "What do each of us owe?", which very strongly suggests that she made a performance error that you avoided – and you have no good reason to give up your judgment that she's your peer on this type of calculation and even this calculation in particular.

In this story you had *two* B beliefs: B1 is "We each owe $43" and B2 is "It isn't true that we each owe $133." The second belief didn't cross your mind before your friend opened her mouth, but you were firmly disposed to accept it. You also had two P beliefs: P1 is "She is my peer on B1" and P2 is "She is my peer on B2." You were very confident in both P1 and P2, though, again, neither of them actually passed through your mind explicitly. But you were even more confident in B2, which made you think she must have made a performance error in her calculation.

Is this really a counterexample to the Peer Rule***? I'm not sure, but I do suspect this: the question is probably not terribly important when it comes to figuring out how to respond to disagreement in real life.

5

When You Have No Idea Who is in the Better Position

Thus far we have been thinking about cases in which you have opinions regarding the Better Position Question: you think you are in a better position to judge B, you think you and those who disagree with you are peers, or you think they are in a better position to judge B. But we all encounter many situations in our lives in which we are aware of a disagreement but have little or no idea who is in a better position to judge B and we don't know what the experts think either.

50 Conflict in Libya

I am a philosopher, not a lawyer. And I don't talk to lawyers about law. But in the summer of 2011 I read two articles which said (a) the US military action in Libya in the summer of 2011 was a war, (b) the USA can't legally go to war unless the US Congress approves it, but (c) the US Congress never approved the war. It's not a surprise that, *if* (a) to (c) is true, *then* the US military action in Libya was illegal. However, what is controversial is the conjunction of (a) to (c), especially (a). The articles seemed pretty convincing to me that (a) to (c) was true, but I know full well that I'm a *total* amateur on the relevant topics and I haven't done *any* research on the matter (and now I *can't* do even a little bit of research, as it will ruin my example!). I have literally no idea what the community of experts think about it, with the possible exception of the two commentators I read. I know that some intelligent and at least mildly informed people agree with me; and I know that some intelligent and at least mildly informed people disagree with me. But I haven't the faintest idea which group is the superior of which, and I have no idea how many people are in each camp.

That is a case in which I know that I am an amateur and I also know that there are genuine experts, but I have no idea what the experts taken as a group think, even though I suspect I know what a few of them think.

51 Psychology Class

You got a certain answer on a mildly difficult question on a homework assignment for a psychology class. Before turning your assignment in, you compare notes with the student who sits next to you. You're not friends but you're acquaintances. You have no real idea what her abilities are when it comes to the assignment, psychology, or intellectual work in general. So you have no idea if she's your peer, superior, or inferior when it comes to the question on the assignment. You then find out she got an answer different from yours but not terribly different.

In this case the experts drop out as irrelevant. You can be pretty sure that the experts, taken as a group, have a definite opinion on the matter, as it's unlikely that your psychology professor gave you a homework problem whose answer is highly controversial among psychologists. But you haven't the foggiest idea what any of the experts think. All you know is what another amateur thinks.

52   Wall Street vs. Main Street

If you keep track of politics at all, then you have heard, over and over, that politicians in many countries are beholden to rich people. The rich fund the campaigns of politicians and supply them with jobs when they and their staff retire from politics; and the rich folks expect returns on their investments. But you have also heard that politician Hennessy doesn't work that way: although she accepts money from rich people and powerful corporations, she works for the interests of common people, not the rich. Unfortunately, you have also heard that this favorable news is just rank propaganda – lies made up and circulated in order to secure support for Hennessy.

In these cases one is faced with uncertainty. You know that there are people who reject your belief, but you have no idea whether they are in a better or worse position than you to judge the matter. Nor do you have any idea how many agree with you, how many disagree with you, how many suspend judgment, how many experts there are, etc. What should you do?

It's tempting to think the right thing to do is just ignore them. After all, what else could you do? If you think to yourself, "Well, I should suspend judgment, as there are lots of people who disagree with me," you would be implicitly assuming that the disagreeing group is a peer or superior of your group – and why should you assume that? On the other hand, it would seem equally foolish to just say to yourself, "Well, I'll just stick with my belief B, as there is no reason to think those people know better than I do": why should you think that you are their superior when you have no evidence for that idea?

Things might change if you could justifiably say, "Well, concerning the person who disagrees with me, there's a 1/3 chance she's my peer, a 1/3 chance she's my inferior, and 1/3 chance she's my superior. So . . ." But you don't know the three possibilities are equally likely: just because there are three possibilities doesn't mean they are equally probable.

Since in these situations you have no idea what to do with the information that there are some people who disagree with you, I wonder whether the best you can do is just move on with your life and not make any adjustment to your beliefs. This is not to say that you should just pretend that no one disagrees with you. You should keep that fact in mind, waiting for further information, such as, "Actually, the people who disagree with me represent the considered view of the genuine experts." So perhaps the lesson in these disagreement situations is this: *don't make any change in your view but adopt an openness, a willingness, to adjust your opinion should relevant information about the disagreeing group come to light.* I can think of just one kind of exception: when you are extremely confident in B, you can probably be reasonable in supposing that it's unlikely that the person who disagrees with you is a "super expert" on B – which is just about the only way her opinion could give you decent reason to suspend judgment on B.

6
Split Experts

The Astrology, Smoking–Cancer, and Global Warming cases are not hard to think about because the experts in each of these cases are united in their assessment. But when it comes to questions about what we should eat or what political or economic policies are best, the experts frequently disagree with one another: they are split. This is a very common situation: for a great many interesting issues usually just a few minutes of exploration on the web will show you that the relevant experts are more or less split. What are we supposed to do when we find that out?

In Part I, I looked at how my students react to highly theoretical and controversial issues, such as those regarding free will and the origins of the universe. I mentioned how many of them don't seem to have full-fledged beliefs: they have something like "intellectual inclinations based on their own reading of just the evidence they are aware of." But many others do have full-fledged beliefs – despite knowing that they are not anywhere *near* being experts on free will, determinism, or the origin of the universe. They appear, at least to me after discussing these matters with them, to subscribe to this rule – applied to *full* belief (so we are setting aside the inclination-by-my-own-lights kind of belief):

> <u>Split Experts Rule</u>: Suppose you believe B and then find out that, although there are lots of experts on the topics relevant to B and those experts have investigated B pretty thoroughly, the experts are split: they have come to no consensus on whether B is true. Some think it's true, some think it's false, and a great many say the evidence is

inconclusive. And the percentage of those who accept B is comparable to the percentage who reject B (so it's not as though ten times as many experts agree with you as disagree with you). If you're aware of all that, then the experts *cancel one another out* (the people who disagree with you are canceled out by those who agree with you) and you are reasonable in keeping your *full* belief B, even if you know that you don't possess any key evidence the experts lack.

Applied to the origin of the universe question from Part I, people who subscribe to the Split Experts Rule think that they are free to take a side – believing either something must have caused the universe to begin or that it began with no such cause – when they learn that the experts taken as a group don't know what to think on the matter. The idea here is that the experts provide a constraint on belief *only* when they agree on some matter; otherwise the constraint is off and one is "free" to believe based on one's own lights.

I think this is half right and half wrong. More precisely, I consider that the rule is useful because thinking about it reveals an important subtlety in the notion of "epistemic reasonableness" on which we have been focusing. First I'll explain why I think the Split Experts Rule is "half wrong." Then, in section 9, I'll tackle the "half-right" portion, the bit that raises the issue of how to interpret the phrase "epistemically reasonable."

The fact that the large group of experts disagree with one another regarding B, even after sharing their evidence and arguing about it for a long time with no consensus, strongly suggests that the *total* body of evidence they have, as a group, is inconclusive: it doesn't show B is true and it doesn't show B is false. Very likely, the total body of evidence contains impressive evidence E1 *for* B as well as impressive evidence E2 *against* B: E1 has convinced some experts to believe B and E2 has convinced other experts to believe not-B. And when you sit there, as an amateur on the outside, and learn of how the experts are split, you should, if you think about it a bit, realize that, although there is good evidence for your view, there is really good evidence against it as well – that's *why* so many experts disagree with you – and you really have no idea which pot of evidence is the stronger one.

Here is another way to think about it. Since you're an amateur regarding B who has reflected on the matter appropriately, the odds are that the experts will already know about whatever evidence you have for B. If you were given a chance to defend B, you wouldn't say anything they haven't heard before. And yet, a great many of those experts, who are familiar with your reasons for B, reject B. That must mean that either they don't think your reasons are very good or they have reasons against B that are very good (after all, you know that these people tend to base their beliefs on the subject matter on evidence, not whim, otherwise they would hardly merit the title "expert"). Regardless of which of the two options is the right one, your reasons for B don't settle the matter.

Now, if you had some special information about the experts, then it might be reasonable to stick with your belief. For instance, you might know that the so-called experts who disagree with you are horribly biased compared to you. But in a great many cases you won't be in a good position to justifiably say anything like that.

Here is a case that illustrates my point.

53   Chocolate and Cancer

Suppose you have heard that chocolate is a good cancer preventative. You've heard it from a friend and read it in two magazines; that's all your evidence. But then you learn that a great many experts have thoroughly studied the issue for many years and they are about evenly split on whether chocolate is a good cancer preventative (the friend and the magazine articles didn't mention any of this controversy). That's all you know about what the experts have said on the matter. You also know that you don't have any evidence regarding chocolate that the nutritionists lack (it's not as though they don't eat chocolate but you do!).

In that scenario it's just obvious that you're unreasonable to retain your full belief that chocolate is a good cancer preventative. You should react to the fact that the experts are split not with, "Good; I can believe whatever I want," but with something like, "Oh man. I guess we don't really know whether chocolate is good for preventing cancer."

None of this is meant to suggest that, *in all cases* when experts disagree on some matter, you need to suspend judgment. If you know that you have key evidence they lack, then the views of experts might not tell you much of anything.

We need to examine the situation more fully. Suppose you found out that the community of experts suspended judgment on B – virtually all of them. You the amateur have belief B, and you have always thought that you had good reason R to think B was true. But now you have found out that almost 100 percent of the sizable community of experts who have considered B have decided neither to believe nor to disbelieve it. B might be the claim "Fifty years from now we'll have flying cars," and the experts are people who study transportation technology and related matters.

In that circumstance you should probably realize that your evidence for B isn't that great. After all, you're no expert and the experts probably know about your so-called good reason R to believe B. And yet, despite knowing about R, they have suspended judgment on B. That very strongly suggests that either R isn't good reason for B or there is some comparable reason R* that says B is false (and in the latter case the experts suspend judgment on B because they think R and R* – as well as other relevant reasons – cancel each other out). Either way, you know this: the *total* evidence lying around, more or less shared by the members of the expert community, doesn't support either B or not-B (since, if it did, the experts would probably be able to see that, given that they are experts). So why on earth would you stick with your belief in B when you have every reason to think that *the total evidence doesn't support B*? Sure, you might be right that *your* bit of evidence supports B, but you will then know that the evidence left over, and possessed by the experts, supports not-B to a significant extent. It would be pretty foolish to think that the evidence you the amateur happen to possess is the legitimate evidence and the rest is misleading.

However, what if you found out that the experts thought differently? Suppose 80 percent of them suspend judgment on B but the other 20 percent accept it? Well, now things are getting more difficult to assess. On the one hand, the fact that a huge percentage of the sizable community of experts has thought about and then suspended judgment on B strongly suggests that the total evidence regarding B is not supportive of B (neither is it supportive of not-B). Then, again, the fact that 20 percent of them agree with you that B is true – and none of them thinks B is false – is a sign that the total evidence does support B! So what should you do with all this information? And what if it wasn't a mere 20 percent who agreed with you but 35 percent? What then?

I don't know. By fiddling with the numbers it's not at all hard to dream up a great many realistic situations in which it is awfully difficult, even after intelligent reflection, to know what the reasonable thing to do is. This fact will lead to my comments on what is "half right" about the Split Experts Rule, which I will present in section 9.

7
Special Case: Religious Belief[7]

The case of religious disagreement is probably the most important one when it comes to consequences, as religious conflict is a large cause of murder, differential treatment, and other things of questionable morality. Recall that there are several questions regarding the rationality of a belief vis-à-vis disagreement: the question whether the belief *started out* reasonable before the realization of disagreement, the question whether the believer's *reaction* to the realization of disagreement is reasonable, and whether her *subsequent* belief (assuming she sticks with her old belief) is reasonable. As mentioned earlier, the second question is our main focus.

In R. Scott Bakker's novel *The Warrior-Prophet*, Achamian is a sorcerer who is occasionally hired by kings to tutor their sons in academic subjects such as history, composition, and mathematics (but not sorcery, the education of which is closely guarded). One of Achamian's students, Prince Proyas, becomes a king as a relatively young man. Achamian is skeptical about the epistemic lives of most people. Proyas, affectionately known as Prosha, grows to be a fervent believer in the established religion of his time and culture. As an adult, he reflects on his childhood education under Achamian.

> Beliefs were the foundation of actions. Those who believed without doubting, he would say, acted without thinking. And those who acted without thinking were enslaved.

[7]Much of this section is taken from my "Religious Disagreement", forthcoming in Graham Oppy (ed.), *Handbook of Contemporary Philosophy of Religion*, Acumen Press (December 2014).

That was what Achamian would say.

Once, after listening to his beloved older brother, Tirum-mas, describe his harrowing pilgrimage to the Sacred Land, Proyas had told Achamian how he wished to become a Shiral Knight.

"Why?" the portly Schoolman [Achamian] had exclaimed. . . .

"So I can kill heathens on the Empire's frontier!"

Achamian tossed his hands skyward in dismay. "Foolish boy! How many faiths are there? How many competing beliefs? And you would *murder* another on the slender hope that yours is somehow the *only* one?"

"Yes! I have *faith*!"

"Faith," the Schoolman repeated, as though recalling the name of a hated foe. "Ask yourself, Prosha . . . What if the choice isn't between certainties, between this faith and that, but between faith and *doubt*? Between renouncing the mystery and embracing it?"

"But doubt is weakness!" Proyas cried. "Faith is strength! Strength!" Never, he was convinced, had he felt so holy as at that moment. The sunlight seemed to shine straight through him, to bathe his heart.

"Is it? Have you looked around you, Prosha? Pay atten-tion, boy. Watch and tell me how many men, out of weakness, *lapse* into the practice of doubt. Listen to those around you, and tell me what you see . . ."

He did exactly as Achamian had asked. For several days, he watched and listened. . . . And in the midst of innumerable boasts, declarations, and accusations, only rarely did he hear those words Achamian had made so familiar, so commonplace . . . The words Proyas himself found so difficult! And even then, they belonged most to those Proyas considered wise, even-handed, compassionate, and least to those he thought stupid or malicious.

"*I don't know.*"

Why were these words so difficult?

"Because men want to murder," Achamian had explained afterward. "Because men want their gold and their glory. Because they want beliefs that *answer* to their fears, their hatreds, and their hungers." (pp. 374–5)

This excerpt contains several ideas regarding our topic. First, Achamian seems to be saying that Proyas would be foolish to be so confident in his religion that he would go and kill the heathens with respect to that religion. Achamian's offered reason for doubt appears to be the diversity of religions. In response, Proyas thinks having faith is justification enough for those murders. He seems to think that one simply must have *some* worthwhile religion, and any worthwhile religion will demand the murder of its opponents. Achamian replies that one does not have to choose among the various murderous religions; agnosticism, which means embracing the mystery of the universe without corresponding belief, or at least murderous belief, is a genuine alternative. Proyas responds with the accusation that such agnosticism goes hand in hand with weakness. Achamian disagrees. Under Achamian's recommendation Proyas then observes that doubt appears to be both favorably linked with wisdom, compassion, and even-handedness and opposed to stupidity and maliciousness. Doubt no longer looks as if it's linked with weakness. Achamian has a harsh diagnosis: those who adopt confident religious beliefs, at least those that recommend murder, do so out of fear, hatred, and hunger – not anything like evidence.

I think every reader of this book will agree with most of what Achamian has to say. One should not be so confident in the truth of a religion that tells one to murder the heathens. If your faith is telling you to bomb an abortion clinic, for instance, it's time to reassess those beliefs, as one needs to be pretty darn sure of one's beliefs before one goes around murdering people.

So much is obvious to enlightened folk, many of whom are happy to adopt less violent religious beliefs. But Achamian's basic point applies to those beliefs as well: how can you justify any religious belief at all, pro *or* con, given that you know full well that there are a great many highly intelligent and well-informed people who reject that belief? The religious belief might be something relatively specific, such as "Jesus rose from the dead," "Salvation occurs only through Jesus," or "The soul is reincarnated." Or it might be something more fundamental, such as "God exists." It could be something scientific, such as "Humans were created in pretty much their present form in the last few thousand years,"

"There is no afterlife for humans," or "The earth was covered in water several thousand years ago." It could also be opposing beliefs: "Jesus didn't rise from the dead," "Salvation can occur through non-Christian means," "God doesn't exist at all," or "Humans evolved over a great many millennia." Even if in *some* cases apparent disagreement is merely apparent (e.g., so-called disagreements about "salvation" might be artifacts of different understandings of that term), it's clear that in an enormous number of cases only one group can be right: either Jesus rose from the dead or he didn't, we either are or are not conscious after the death of our bodies, and either a person created the physical universe or no one did. In each case, if you aren't culturally sheltered then you are perfectly aware that there are many very intelligent people who disagree with you. What makes you think you and your co-believers are right and all those other folks are wrong? Is your group smarter or more careful in its reasoning? Does your group have key evidence the other group lacks – and if you think that's the case, then how do you know they don't have key evidence that you lack? Has your group evaded some bit of irrationality that infects the other group? If you think your group has got the issue right, and everyone who disagrees has got it wrong, you probably think that your group has some epistemic advantage the other group fails to have – but do you?

Anyone who has come this far in the book knows it can be difficult to be rationally confident in answering those questions in the previous paragraph in a way that reflects happily on oneself. In particular, it will often be difficult if you are familiar with the diversity, and epistemic credentials of members, of religious viewpoints. Suppose I have the following beliefs: God exists, Jesus is God, and some of us have eternal life in Heaven. I know perfectly well that there are a great many philosophers who have examined the publicly available evidence for these claims and have found it highly defective; indeed, many think the evidence against my beliefs is very strong. In fact, I'm aware that a clear majority have this skeptical view about my religious beliefs. I am not oblivious, living under a rock; and I am not in denial, fooling myself with wishful thinking. I know perfectly well that my religious beliefs are highly controversial in the uncomfortable way: they are denied by a great number and percentage of the *best thinkers around* who have studied the publicly available information that might be relevant to the rational assessment of my beliefs.

Despite all this, I think it's pretty clear that a great many people are utterly reasonable in sticking to their beliefs in the face of religious disagreement – in one familiar sense of "reasonable." We have seen plenty of test cases that can make the general point. For instance, a child with religious belief B might be told by her parents and *all* the other people she looks up to that, although there are people who doubt or even reject B, they are screwed up in any of various ways: horribly irrational, biased, brainwashed, ignorant, insane, etc. She believes them on this score; why on earth would she not do so, given that she is sheltered from reality, she has always unreflectively trusted those adults, and those adults have proven reliable about so many issues before? She has a false belief – it's far from true that all those people are screwed up in those ways – but she is completely reasonable in accepting it and then, as a consequence, keeping her belief in B. Nothing relevant changes if the believer is a sheltered adult instead of a child. Nor is this verdict dependent on the belief being a pro-religious one: it applies to atheism and other anti-religious views.

Those are the easy cases. Of course, we still have the task of telling an informative story about the kind of reasonability in question – the kind that applies to the child's sticking with her belief in B. The kind of reasonableness she has means we can't truthfully accuse her with the charges "She should know better" and "If she doesn't change her view, then she's being foolish." The child has strong testimony that there is good experiential, scientific, or philosophical evidence for her religious beliefs; more simply, she just has strong testimony for the truth of her theistic beliefs. Note that the testimony suffices for an ordinary type of epistemic reasonableness in her beliefs *independently of the testimony's origin*, where the origin might be someone who directly perceived God but also might be someone who was insane and deluded. For comparison, even if the whole idea of electrons and protons is a stunningly successful and long-running gag perpetrated by generations of twisted physicists and chemists, it remains true that, in ordinary senses of "testimony" and "epistemically reasonable," we non-scientists have excellent testimony for our shared belief that atoms contain electrons and protons – testimony good enough to make our belief reasonable in an epistemically robust manner.

The topic of religious disagreement gets most interesting when the believer isn't sheltered. She need not actually *meet* anyone who disagrees with her. Instead, her problems often begin with a simple train of thought that can be expressed as follows.

> Wait a minute. There are loads of religions out there: dozens and dozens if you separate different kinds of Christianity, Buddhism, etc. They can't all be right: they conflict in many ways. If the Catholics are right about X, then the Protestants are wrong about X and the Buddhists are so far off it's almost comical. How do I know mine is the right one? I think Jesus rose from the dead; lots of other people say he didn't; we can't both be right! Of all the dozens of religious views out there, how do I know I've managed to latch on to the right one? Is it okay [practically? morally? epistemically?] for me just to *have faith* or *hope* that I've got the true one?

As soon as one is well aware of and reflects seriously on the diversity of religious opinion, pro and con, one is put in what looks to be an epistemically uncomfortable position. *If* one manages rationally to come to think that the folks on the other side are the epistemic inferiors to the folks on one's home team (one's home team is the people who share one's belief), *then* one usually can be reasonable in retaining one's religious belief. For instance, I am rationally confident that Hell is not located in the center of Earth, even though that belief might be quite controversial among ten-year-olds who have been brought up in certain primitive religious communities. The problem, of course, is that, the more worldly one becomes, the harder it is always to think rationally that one's home team has the advantage over the people one disagrees with. And please keep in mind that this applies to atheists as well as theists.

Let's look a little more carefully at how awareness of religious disagreement usually comes about, focusing on pro-religious belief. In most cases one acquires the pro-religious belief B via testimony when one is young, where (i) the testimony comes from people one would regard as one's superiors on the matter (for one thing, they are adults) and (ii) one learns pretty quickly that *a great many people* have that belief B, usually including many people one would judge to be one's epistemic superiors on the belief. It is usually later that one learns of people who disbelieve B, and this realization has several distinct stages. First, one learns of other religions – ones that differ from one's own. That's stage 1. Next, one learns that these other religions have different beliefs: whereas mine has beliefs B1 and B2, that other one has beliefs B3 and B4. That's stage 2. Note that these are different stages: there could be religions that differed in numerous significant ways but had the same beliefs. (In fact, I suspect that many people don't consider beliefs to be central to religions.) Third, one learns that the other religion denies what one's own religion affirms: we think their B3 is false and they think our B1 is false. That's stage 3. So, finally, the person becomes aware of religious disagreement as such: we can't all be right in our religious beliefs, so someone is wrong. These stages might all occur in one conversation, but, then again, their unfolding might occur over a span of years; it depends on the child's intellectual sophistication and curiosity, as well as on the remarks of her conversational participants. And when one learns about the disagreement, one typically learns that there are *a great many* people who disbelieve B (e.g., one learns of multiple *world* religions). When you disagree with your sister about which relative played the piano at your grandmother's house when you were little children, there is a *disagreement-with-one* case; religious disagreement is virtually always a *disagreement-with-many* case.

Finally, after reaching stage 3, one *can* proceed to stage 4, characterized by the "Wait a minute" speech above – but this doesn't always happen. Even at stage 3, the problem of religious disagreement might not arise with much force. A great many Catholics, for instance, will acknowledge that there are millions of people who think the central tenets of Catholicism are false, but *no reflection at all* goes along with that knowledge. The same holds for other faiths of course. (This can be difficult to comprehend for philosophers, since they are hyper-reflective.) Only when the "Wait a minute: how do we know we're right and they're wrong?" attitude passes through one's consciousness with some force does the epistemic challenge become acute – or at least has the *potential* for being such.

If my students (at Fordham University, which has academically inclined students) are at all representative, then the "Wait a minute" stage 4 of awareness is fairly uncommon. For what it's worth, when I teach the topic I encounter a large percentage of students who, by their atypical blank stares, have clearly not reached stage 4, even though they have managed to reach stage 3. Just because the challenge of religious disagreement has been served on a silver platter does not mean that people will catch a whiff of it. From now on I will address only those people who have reached the "Wait a minute" stage 4 of awareness and reflection.

As we have seen, one natural thing to do upon reflecting on disagreement is to wonder whether your group has some advantage over the disagreeing group. For instance, I might think Jesus is the Messiah because I think Christians "know something others have missed," where that phrase indicates some crucial piece of evidence (e.g., I think Christians have had personal experiences of Jesus that suggest he's the Messiah).

However, it's not true that, in all cases of reflective religious disagreement, the person who keeps her belief after significant reflection thinks that her group is better positioned to judge B. As we saw in the beginning of Part II of this book, there are several categories of cases to consider for the person who reaches stage 4.

Category 1: You have never thought at all, even implicitly, about the issue of who is better positioned to judge B correctly.

Category 2: You have thought about it but realize that you have no idea whose position is better.

Category 3: You think you have (or your group has) the overall better epistemic position.

Category 4: You think they have the overall better epistemic position.

Category 5: You think the two positions are about equal.

In this section I will examine only categories 3 and 5, starting with the latter.

Recently there have been works written on peer disagreement by instantiating B with various religious claims (e.g., Kraft 2012, Feldman 2007, Oppy 2010, Thune 2010, DePoe 2011, Lackey 2014, Bogardus 2013). Although these cases are theoretically interesting, in my view it is tricky to apply the theoretical issues of interest to epistemologists to the *real-life* cases of religious disagreement. There are several primary reasons for this, each of which throws light on the epistemology of the types of religious disagreement that are actually most common.

First, most of the pressing cases of religious disagreements are many-on-many, not one-on-one, as is suggested by the recent epistemology literature. If I'm Jewish and I wonder whether the Christians are right about Jesus being the Messiah, I'm going to consider whether *we Jews* have some evidence or some other factor that gives us an advantage over *the Christians*. I won't be concerned whether *I* happen to have an advantage over *my neighbor* who is Lutheran.

Second, in an enormous number of cases people think, at least implicitly, that their group is in a better position to judge B. I will think that my group knows something the critics have missed (e.g., we Christians have experienced Jesus in a certain epistemically fruitful way; we atheists understand science and critical thinking better than theists). So an enormous number of religious disagreements won't be recognized peer cases on either an individual *or* a group basis. In another large number of cases, people realize that they have no idea which group is better positioned (e.g., on how to interpret the book of Genesis). Hence, focusing on the peer category makes one miss the enormous number of cases in the other categories. And don't forget the many millions of people who don't reflect at all on the fact of disagreement, beyond merely noting that religions disagree on some matters. In my judgment the peer category is small compared to the others.

Third, for the central religious belief – "God exists" – it's arguable that the vast majority of people will insist that they are in the better position to judge the belief (and as a result these disagreements will fall into category 3, not 5). A great many theists will think that the atheists are just missing out on experiencing God; the atheists will generally think the theists have let any of a variety of epistemic weaknesses infect their judgment. I'll examine this case in the next section.

Fourth, although there are cases of peer disagreement when it comes to religion, the notion of peerhood has to be extremely loose, allowing for a great deal of difference in the two groups, in order for there to be a significant number of category 5 cases. For instance, two disagreeing theists might consider themselves peers over whether Jesus really raised anyone from the dead, whether an afterlife Heaven really exists, whether evolution is true, whether God is really perfectly good, whether God ever changes, whether salvation occurs through Jesus or other means, whether the pope's decisions and views are substantially influenced by God, etc. However, in those real-life cases I doubt whether people often have any opinion regarding "peerhood" beyond that expressed by, "Well, I figure we're very roughly equal." They probably won't think the two groups have the *same evidence* or are equal on other epistemically relevant factors, such as time devoted to the issue, intellectual ability, relevant background knowledge, and circumstances of investigation. How would anyone ever have good reason to think two groups are about equal on those factors when it comes to religious beliefs? Not only that: it's not difficult to realize that humans are extremely diverse in their exposure to arguments, experiences, and evidence, pro and con, regarding religious claims; they are also diverse in general intellectual qualities; finally, the amount of time spent in relevant reflection will vary greatly as well (in addition to varying in qualities such as intensity).

People who fall into category 3 think their group is in a much better position to judge B. If, after going through stage 4, I come firmly to believe that my group is in a much better position to judge whether B is true, then, as we have seen, by and large it will be reasonable for me to stick with my belief B as a consequence of making that comparative judgment. So it's arguable that the answer to the Disagreement Question in this kind of case will be "Yes." This kind of situation breaks down into two species: my belief in my group's superiority *is or is not* well supported by my overall evidence. In the "is" case, it seems pretty clear that, at least in most situations, my retaining B will be reasonable.

We have looked at stories that suggest that the same might be true for the "is not" case. To be sure, the person who sticks with B when *unreasonably* thinking her group is in the superior position has made an epistemic error; that's logically true ("unreasonable" entails "epistemic error"). But her error isn't in the retaining of the belief: it's in the *prior* judgment of superiority. *Given that* she has made the unreasonable judgment of superiority, the reasonable thing for her to do next, in updating her position on B, is to keep B. If someone believes B, she knows that many others disbelieve B, she is quite convinced that she has absolutely key evidence that the others lack, and she is convinced that the others have no relevant epistemic advantage over her, then she would be irrational to suspend judgment just because those people disagree with her. The rational thing for her to do is stick with her belief, even though her *retained belief* in B will still be irrational. Her *overall* dealings with the disagreement are flawed, but the flaw happened *before* the retaining of belief B. This is similar to the Japan stories described earlier.

Hence, if one has an unreasonable judgment about epistemic superiority, this judgment might make reasonable one's sticking with one's belief in the face of disagreement – although one's overall dealings with disagreement contain important irrationalities. I suspect this is true and a common occurrence: a great many people do indeed have unjustified beliefs in epistemic superiority when it comes to religious beliefs, pro and con. For instance, many atheists are confident that theists just don't understand much of anything about science or reason. Of course, there is *some* truth to this: many adult theists, at least in the USA, are young Earth creationists, even though they are intelligent enough to know that that position is idiotic. But a great many theists are quite familiar with science and reason, to put it mildly, and atheists rarely have much reason to think all, or even almost all, theists are fools about science or reason (and, when they do, it's testimonial and they are living a sheltered life). So, their judgment of superiority is usually unjustified. On the other side, theists often too quickly believe that their experiences of seeing the starry skies or the birth of a baby provide excellent evidence for various theistic claims (e.g., "Jesus understands and loves me"): they have little reason to accept such an idea and often have decent evidence that such a belief might be the product of wishful thinking or something similarly epistemically defective.

So judgments of epistemic superiority are often unjustified. Whether they are true is a controversial matter in a great many real-life cases. For instance, reflective theists often claim C_T that many of them experience God in such a way as to generate justified theistic beliefs and then transmit reasonableness to other theists via testimony. These alleged perceptions make up a diverse class: a dramatic cognitive "lightning bolt" sent from God (think of the account in Acts of St Paul's experiences on the road to Damascus), an enlightenment experience as the result of years of disciplined meditation, the witnessing of something common but extraordinarily moving such as the birth of a baby, or a more general perception that results from reflecting on one's overall life, allegedly seeing God guiding one in subtle ways that will usually not be convincing to outsiders. On the other hand, atheists often claim C_A that all theistic belief is grounded in some combination of wishful thinking, groupthink, testimony that is poorly grounded, fatally flawed arguments, and other factors excluding perception and impressive scientific or philosophical evidence.

Needless to say, both C_T and C_A are highly controversial. My main point here is that, *if* someone believed either claim, C_T or C_A, *then* they would fall into category 3; and, *if* they did fall into that category, then it's plausible to think that the answer to the Disagreement Question would be affirmative for them whether or not C_T or C_A was justified for them.

The fact that many people embrace the two claims, C_T and C_A, shows two more things: first, that there are a great many category 3 cases, as was mentioned above; and, second, how certain fundamental epistemological questions about religious belief – C_T and C_A, for instance – are important when evaluating how reasonable it is to stick with one's religious beliefs in the face of reflective disagreement.

I will close this section with a few all too brief comments on the other area of extensive and important disagreement: politics. There are similarities in religious and political beliefs, but they differ in some key ways that matter when it comes to the epistemology of disagreement.[8]

First, there is a great deal of verifiable information directly relevant to political belief. There are all sorts of facts and figures directly relevant to how such-and-such political initiatives fared. Whether or not people are *aware* of these facts and figures is a separate issue. This is different from the case of religion.

Second, there is much more intentional dishonesty in political discourse. When one religious person says Jesus rose from the dead and another says he didn't, in virtually all cases neither person is intentionally lying to us: each person firmly believes that he or she is telling the truth. Only one is right, but both sincerely *think* they are right. But in politics the opposite happens all the time: people in the public eye say things they know are false. I'll give examples from recent politics in the USA.

For instance, many people who work for Fox News Corporation will say that it is not a propaganda arm of the Republican Party even though they know full well that what they are saying is false. Another example: a great many Republican politicians will say the very opposite of what they know when it comes to science. For instance, they will say either that global warming doesn't exist or, if it does, is minor and not caused by the use of fossil fuels. They know these statements are false, but they say them anyway for various practical reasons. Many people in the Democratic Party will say that President Barack Obama's record on civil rights is quite different from George W. Bush's record, even though they know better. In addition, many will say that the Obama administration applies the same legal rules to rich and powerful people as to others, even though they are aware that it just ain't so. I don't want to deny that there are many "true believers": Fox News staff who genuinely believe that their

---

[8] There were some interesting thoughts on political disagreement in a couple of recent articles by Gary Gutting in the *New York Times*, available online at: http://opinionator.blogs.nytimes.com/.

news programs are "fair and balanced," Republican politicians who actually believe that global warming doesn't exist, and Democratic Party operatives who really think that Obama is significantly more protective and respectful of civil rights than the previous presidential administration. But the amount of dishonesty in public discourse is simply staggering and – importantly – socially acceptable.

Third, although there is a great deal of public debate about various political positions – unlike religious positions – much of this debate is devoid of evidence and reason. The point in the previous paragraph about dishonesty is just one way in which most political discourse is subpar. But if the public epistemic standards for political discourse are really, *really* low, as I suspect is the case, then perhaps the standards for reasonable belief formation and retention are also low.

8
Some Results

As I did in Part I, I will list some results we have come up with in Part II, continuing the numbering from before. Then I will proceed to address some tough questions that we definitely do *not* yet have answers for.

27 When it's reasonable to retain your old belief, we say that it's reasonable to be **steadfast** in your view; when you have to suspend judgment *or* adopt the other person's view, we say that one has to be **conciliatory**. So, there are two importantly different ways to be conciliatory.

28 When you realize that you disagree with someone or some group over claim B, there are several categories you can fall into, depending on your thoughts on the Better Position Question:

- Category 1: You have never thought at all, even implicitly, about the issue of who is better positioned to judge B correctly.
- Category 2: You have thought about it but realize that you have no idea whose position is better.
- Category 3: You think you have (or your group has) the overall better epistemic position.
- Category 4: You think they have the overall better epistemic position.
- Category 5: You think the two positions are about equal.

29 The Smoking–Cancer and Astrology stories put pressure on the Peer Rule; the Global Warming story puts

pressure on the Superior Rule; and the Doctors and Doctors story suggests the falsity of the Controversy Rule. In addition, those stories help motivate the Peer Rule*, the Superior Rule*, and the Controversy Rule*.

30 The Holiday Piano Peer I and Group Projects I stories put pressure on the Peer Rule*. The crucial factor seems to be the *disparity* between one's overall evidence for B and one's overall evidence for P: when the former vastly outweighs the latter, it's reasonable to keep one's belief B in the face of disagreement.

31 The Holiday Piano Superior story suggests that the Superior Rule* is false: when you are massively more confident in B than in S, then it can be reasonable to stick with B. However, it's not true that if you're totally, completely confident in B then you get to stick with your belief regardless of disagreement: the Awareness of Astronomy and Awareness of Atheism cases showed this.

32 The Quad story (and variants) also seem to refute the Peer Rule* and the Superior Rule*.

33 In some cases, such as the Astrology one, the reasonable thing to do is give up P while retaining B, but in other cases, such as the Restaurant Bill II story, one should retain both P and B. So, keeping B doesn't *always* mean giving up P.

34 The Ritalin, Group Projects II, and New Software II stories give us some evidence that the Peer Rule** and Superior Rule** are false. They also motivate the *** versions of those rules.

35 However, there is evidence that the *** rules are false as well, as the Restaurant Bill II story suggested.

36 The Split Experts Rule is probably false. However, it is easy to think of cases in which one learns detailed facts about expert opinion but it isn't at all clear what the body of evidence means, even for someone who is intelligent and puts some thought into the matter.

37 There are a great many religious beliefs, pro and con, and they make a diverse collection. Examples: "Jesus rose from the dead," "Salvation occurs only through Jesus,"

"The soul is reincarnated," "God exists," "Humans were created in pretty much their present form in the last few thousand years," "There is no afterlife for humans," or "The Earth was covered in water several thousand years ago."

38 Testimony from a great many people and books can make one's pro-religious beliefs reasonable in one common sense of "reasonable." Matters get epistemically interesting when the believer learns of the extent to which people disagree with her religious views.

39 One typically goes through a sequence of stages of awareness of religious disagreement:

> Stage 1: One learns of other religions – ones that differ from one's own.
> Stage 2: One learns that these other religions have different beliefs: whereas mine has beliefs B1 and B2, that other one has beliefs B3 and B4.
> Stage 3: One learns that the other religion denies what one's own religion affirms: we think their B3 is false and they think our B1 is false. So, finally, the person becomes aware of religious disagreement as such: we can't all be right in our religious beliefs, so someone is wrong.
> Stage 4: One thinks to oneself something along the lines of the "Wait a minute" thought.

40 A person who reaches stage 4 with respect to her religious belief B will fall into one of five categories described in point (28) above.

41 Most cases of religious disagreement are many-on-many, not one-on-one.

42 Most cases of religious disagreement have each party falling into categories 1 or 3 from point (28) above.

43 In order for a significant number of cases to fall into category 5, the notion of peerhood will have to be very loose.

44 If a person falls into category 3, then their belief retention could be reasonable even if their belief that they fall into that category is unjustified.

45 Whether a given person's belief that she falls into category 3 is true is often highly controversial.

I call points (27) to (45) "results" because I'm fairly confident that they are true or at least close to being true (e.g., notice that in many cases all they say are things like "it *seems* that X").

9
Questions on Uniqueness, Independence, and Peerhood

Now we will proceed to address some tough epistemological questions – ones that generate a lot of expert disagreement. I start by revisiting the split experts cases, as they will be key to addressing these new questions.

I think that, when faced with the various "experts are split or undecided" scenarios described earlier in section 6 – as well as many more you can probably think of yourself – most of us are not good at judging them. When faced with challenges such as "One third of them agree with B, one third disagree with B, and one third suspend judgment: what's the reasonable thing to do in response?," most of us don't have the ability to figure out what to say. For what it's worth, when I've presented these cases to philosophers, I have had several quite intelligent ones react with "Stick with your belief," while others were confident with "Suspend judgment." This suggests to me that it's pretty difficult to figure out how to respond to the various experts-split scenarios. Surprisingly enough, a person can be utterly fantastic at acquiring and thinking through an extremely complicated body of evidence E1 that is directly relevant to B (e.g., experimental evidence regarding a very complicated theory in physics) and yet be pretty awful at thinking through a body of evidence E2 about E1. It's almost like being faced with a difficult logical puzzle.

There are two very fancy, expensive treasure chests, one covered all in gold and the other covered all in silver. Exactly one contains a marvelous treasure. The gold one bears on its cover the words "The treasure is not in here"; the silver one bears on its cover the words "Exactly one of the two sentences on the covers of the two chests is true." Can you figure out which chest has the treasure?

There is a definite right answer here – and it's *not* the one people first come to when they try to solve it by logic alone – but it's hard to find it even though all one really needs to do is think hard about it. Perhaps something similar holds for the various experts-are-split scenarios.

If I'm trying to answer the question "What is the reasonable thing for me to do in such-and-such disagreement situation?" and as a matter of brute fact my evidence definitely points in a certain direction (e.g., towards suspension of judgment), it can be quite difficult for me to figure that out even if I do my best, I'm generally smart, and I carry out my task in an intelligent manner. Given this difficulty, if the evidence says I should suspend judgment but as far as I can determine I'm reasonable in keeping my belief, then in some epistemic sense of "reasonable" I probably *am* reasonable to retain my belief and not suspend judgment as long as I don't have anything like wishful thinking infecting my reasoning. We aren't epistemic gods; the rules that apply to them probably don't apply to us.

Furthermore, it might not be much easier for *an observer* to figure out what I should do. When the observer is figuring out the answer, she will have to juggle various factors:

- What are the strengths of his overall bodies of evidence for B, P, and D?
- What are his confidence levels in B, P, and D?
- How good is he at figuring out the directions in which his overall evidence points?
- How complicated are the facts regarding the directions in which his overall evidence points?

Here is another example that shows how difficult it can be to judge a pot of evidence. Suppose you have a certain body of evidence for your belief. Now consider two scenarios: in one you learn of someone who disagrees with you, has all your evidence, has no more evidence, and is *a bit* smarter than you; in the other scenario, you learn of someone who disagrees with you, has all your evidence, has no more evidence, and is *a lot* smarter than you. So the only difference in the two cases is how much smarter she is compared to you. Presumably, you should adjust your view on the belief in question more in the second case than in the first case. But how much? Good luck figuring that out.

So . . . what are we to make of all this? For starters, these confusing situations seem to be relevantly similar to the ones we went over in section 6, in which you have no real idea what the experts think or whether the people who disagree with you are your superiors, inferiors, or peers on the issue at hand. In both cases you're aware of disagreement but you don't have an inkling of what it means or what to do about it: in the section 6 scenarios you suffer from ignorance of the relevant facts, whereas here you suffer from not knowing what the facts mean.

Uniqueness

I bring these difficult cases up here because the above considerations should make us wary of some key theoretical principles many epistemologists have proposed when thinking about disagreement. Here are a couple of them:

<u>Uniqueness1</u>: If two people have the very same body of evidence, and if they adopt different attitudes towards B (the attitudes: believe it, disbelieve it, or suspend judgment on it), then only one of those attitudes is reasonable. In other words, a pot of evidence can't make two opposing attitudes reasonable: if the evidence shows that belief is reasonable, for instance, then disbelief and suspension can't also be reasonable given the exact same evidence.

<u>Uniqueness2</u>: If two people have the very same body of evidence, and if they adopt different confidence levels in B

(100 percent confidence to 0 percent confidence), then only one of those attitudes is reasonable.[9]

The latter is a more nuanced version of the former, since it allows for not just three attitudes regarding B but many different confidence levels in B's truth.

A point of clarification is in order. We know that if one person believes B while the other disbelieves B, then one of them has a false belief (since they can't both be right). But just because at least one of them has a false belief doesn't mean that they have an unreasonable belief, since not all false beliefs are unreasonable (and not all true beliefs are reasonable). Uniqueness, in other words, is *not* about the truth or falsity of a belief. That's a different notion. Uniqueness, instead, is about the reasonableness of a belief.

The basic idea of Uniqueness is somewhat intuitive. After all, suppose you have a certain pot of evidence E. You think E offers excellent support for belief B. For instance, suppose B is the claim that the cook murdered the maid. Here is the pot of evidence you've got:

a) The cook was seen "hitting on" the maid on several occasions by several witnesses. The witnesses report that the maid flat out rejected him each time.

b) The cook's diary has multiple entries regarding the maid. They start off positive, with descriptions of how much he loves her. But over time (after the rejections) they devolve into rants about the maid, saying all sorts of awful things about her. Two days before the maid's death, there is an entry about how the cook would "love to take a knife to her throat."

---

[9]This principle is somewhat contrived because, for virtually any real belief, we don't have precise confidence levels. This even holds for some beliefs in probabilities. If you give me a pair of dice and ask me what the odds are that when I throw them they will add up to two ("snake eyes"), I will be very confident the answer is *approximately but not exactly* 1/36, as I know full well that the dice probably aren't perfectly made, and so the probabilities will be off a bit (the answer would be exactly 1/36 if the dice were perfect, but of course no dice are perfect).

c) The cook had a long history of violence, with two recent arrests for disorderly conduct while fighting in a pub.
d) The coroner testified that the maid was killed with a long knife.
e) The cook had access to the long kitchen knives.
f) The coroner testified that the murderer was definitely left-handed and used a long knife to make a huge fatal wound. She testified that only a strong left-hander could have done it.
g) The cook was very strong and left-handed.
h) Although the butler is a suspect in the murder and was being blackmailed by the maid, he had a very weak left arm, was right-handed, had no history of violence, and didn't have access to the long kitchen knives.

Suppose you think (a) to (h) offer strong support for B. It would be odd, advocates of Uniqueness say, if two competent people could understand all of (a) to (h) (and no other evidence) and yet one reasonably thinks that it shows that B is true while the other reasonably thinks it shows that B is false. Sure, it's not hard imagining two people having *slightly different* opinions regarding how much (a) to (h) supports B; that's easy to imagine and might show that Uniqueness2 is false. What is hard to imagine, they say, is two people coming to very different yet reasonable opinions regarding B *on the basis of (a) to (h) alone* (clearly, if the two people had extra evidence that was crucially different, then it might turn out that they are both reasonable in their opposite opinions). That's why Uniqueness1 is plausible.

The principle is also *important* because some version of Uniqueness has got to be right. Consider the alternative. If it's entirely false, then you could be completely rational in gazing at the relevant evidence and concluding that B is true while I look at the very same evidence and rationally conclude that B is false. If that's the way things are, then it sure looks as though evidence is no reliable guide to truth, even approximately. But it's hard to see what evidence could be, at all, if it isn't a reliable guide to the truth: isn't it just part of the definition of "evidence" that it is a reliable guide to truth?

Since the Disagreement Question concerns not the status of the *retained belief* but the *retention* of that belief, we need yet another Uniqueness principle. Suppose Ron and Don both come to believe B on the same body of evidence. Each agrees that Jones, some third party, is his or her peer on B (we could treat the case of superior disagreement as well). Then Ron and Don realize that Jones disagrees with B. (Ron and Don don't know anything about each other; they just know about themselves and Jones.) Our third Uniqueness principle says that it can't happen that Ron and Don respond to the disagreement in different yet reasonable ways – for instance, with Ron being reasonable in keeping B and Don being reasonable in suspending judgment on B.[10]

> **Uniqueness3:** If two people start out believing B and P/S regarding a third party (P/S would be "The third party is my peer/superior when it comes to judging B"), come to acquire the new belief D regarding that third party ("The third party disagrees with me regarding B"), and have, at that time, *the very same* total body of evidence regarding all three of B, D, and P/S, then, if they respond differently to the acquisition of belief D (the responses: retain B, reject B, or suspend judgment on B), only one of them is reasonable.

As they are stated above, I think the principles need further refinement since, while the two people in question have the same evidence, they may differ in some Disagreement Factors, such as the amount of time spent thinking about the evidence or the number and "loudness" of distractions encountered in such deliberation. If they do differ in those ways, then perhaps they could reasonably react differently to the disagreement. Therefore, in what follows, let us suppose that the two people are equal not only in evidence but in the other Disagreement Factors as well.

Even with that qualification, we have seen a few cases that can be modified in such a way that we end up putting pressure on Uniqueness3. For instance, suppose someone has

---

[10] There is nothing odd about Ron and Don being reasonable in responding differently to the disagreement with Jones *provided they start out with different reasons for holding B.* But in our story they have the same exact reasons for B, P, and D.

unimpressive overall evidence for B but excellent overall evidence for P. Then she learns of the disagreement, coming to have excellent overall evidence for D. What it's reasonable for her to do at this point depends on her various confidence levels. If she was only mildly confident in B but very confident in both P and D (e.g., if we asked her for her views before the discovery of the disagreement, she would say that she's about 60 percent confident in B but 100 percent confident in P), it seems as though the reasonable thing for her to do is significantly reduce her confidence in B. But if she was 100 percent confident in B and only 60 percent confident in P – so she has misjudged them both – then it seems that the reasonable thing for her to do is keep B and conclude that either P is false or the person she disagrees with made a performance error. Sure, in the latter scenario she has been epistemically naughty, but the naughtiness happened before her discovery of the disagreement: she misjudged the force of her evidence for B and P. We have here two people with the very same evidence (and other Disagreement Factors) who respond to disagreement in different yet reasonable ways. If that's right, Uniqueness3 is false.

Here is an alternative principle that gets around that problem (and, like Uniqueness3, is geared to disagreement):

> **Uniqueness4**: If two people start out believing B and P/S regarding a third party, come to acquire the new belief D regarding that third party, and have, at that time, the very same levels of confidence regarding all three of B, D, and P/S (so their confidence levels in B are the same, their confidence levels in P are the same, etc.), then, if they respond differently to the acquisition of belief D (the responses: retain B, reject B, or suspend judgment on B), only one of them is reasonable.

However, cases like those involving split experts make me doubt even this principle. I can imagine two people who fit the description in Uniqueness4 and who try hard to figure out how to respond to the disagreement in a reasonable way, and yet one thinks she should suspend judgment on B while the other thinks it's okay for her to stick with B – and they come to these differing conclusions because the case is so damn complicated. Perhaps this means that one of them isn't *perfectly* rational – but none of us is perfectly rational.

The first two Uniqueness principles also have troubles with cases of complicated evidence such as the split experts ones. And I can't resist giving a new example, a highly ironic one: appeal to a disagreement amongst philosophers regarding disagreements![11]

We have two philosophers, Stead (for "steadfast") and Concil (for "conciliatory"), who are thinking about a case involving two characters, Yari and Dari. Suppose Yari has overall evidence E_B for his belief B (B could be anything you like). He thinks Dari is his epistemic peer regarding B; that's his belief P. Yari has overall evidence E_P for his belief P. Let's assume that both of those beliefs, the B one and the P one, are strongly supported by the corresponding bodies of evidence E_B and E_P. Then Yari acquires belief D, that Dari disagrees with him over B; and he has overall evidence E_D for the new D belief. Further, the D belief is strongly supported by E_D. So Yari is doing everything right: he has excellent overall evidence for all three of his beliefs.

Stead and Concil agree that Yari has overall evidence $E_B + E_P + E_D$. Philosopher Stead thinks that $E_B + E_P + E_D$ strongly supports retained belief B; so Stead thinks that, if Yari retains B, the retained belief will be evidentially justified. Philosopher Concil thinks that $E_B + E_P + E_D$ does not strongly support retained belief B; so Concil thinks that, if Yari retains B, the retained belief will not be evidentially justified. Alternatively, we could say that Stead and Concil are disagreeing over how Yari should, epistemically, react to the disagreement with Dari – and not merely what his evidence for B comes to – and they are factoring in not just the three bodies of evidence but the confidence levels that Yari has in his three beliefs.

For my purposes here, it matters *not at all* what reasons the two philosophers give for these differing philosophical opinions (the opinions: "B is/isn't epistemically justified" and "Retaining B is/isn't epistemically justified"). It doesn't even

[11] In fact, the cook/maid/butler story might work here as well: two people could look at (a) to (h) and come to reasonable yet different opinions of B based solely on those points.

matter which of them is right. What matters is this: here we have two philosophers who have been thinking quite expertly about epistemological issues for many years who disagree about the strength of $E_B + E_P + E_D$. One says "It strongly supports B" while the other says "It doesn't strongly support B"; one says "It makes retaining B reasonable" while the other says "It makes retaining B unreasonable." Presumably, one of the two philosophers is mistaken (as they are coming to opposite conclusions), but, given the considerable philosophical difficulties involved and the considerable amount of intelligent thought each philosopher has put into the issue, it seems that both philosophers are reasonable in their differing beliefs:

Yari's total evidence strongly supports retained belief B.
Yari's total evidence fails to strongly support retained belief B.

Yari's total evidence strongly supports his retaining belief B.
Yari's total evidence fails to strongly support his retaining belief B.

And if both philosophers are reasonable in their differing beliefs, then surely it follows that *Yari himself* would be reasonable in any of his possible beliefs about himself:

My total evidence strongly supports retained belief B.
My total evidence fails to strongly support retained belief B.

My total evidence strongly supports retaining belief B.
My total evidence fails to strongly support retaining belief B.

And if Yari would be reasonable in having those beliefs, then it sure seems as though both of his possible attitudes regarding B or the retaining of B – belief and suspension, retaining or not – would be reasonable as well. That is, if he's reasonable in thinking "My total evidence strongly supports B/ retaining B," then he is reasonable in believing B/retaining B based on his total evidence. Given the considerable difficulty of the task of figuring out what his evidence says, it would be over the top to *blame* him for adopting the attitude that is not supported by his total evidence. If so, then Uniqueness 1–3 are false, at least for a certain kind of epistemic reasonability tied to blame and praise.

When I say that Yari's possible attitudes of belief or suspension towards B are each *epistemically reasonable*, I am not saying that both are *evidentially supported* by $E_B + E_P + E_D$. This latter claim might be true but it might not; I don't know. If it turns out that only one of those two attitudes concerning B was evidentially supported by his overall evidence, then I think that that would mean that "evidentially supported" is pretty different from "epistemically reasonable," as it would mean that some attitudes are epistemically reasonable even though not evidentially supported.

The point of going over potential counterexamples to the uniqueness principles is not to *refute* those principles – that's too tall an order in the confines of an introductory book – but to *understand better* the issues they raise. That's true also for another potential counterexample, one concerning differing "starting points" and targeted at Uniqueness4.

Suppose Pro and Con disagree about belief B: Pro thinks it's true and Con suspends judgment on it. Pro and Con differ significantly in their background – not in their background *beliefs* but in their background *tendencies*. Pro is the type of person who naturally puts a high value on new ideas, new theories, new possibilities, and new truths. She is *epistemically adventurous*, so to speak. Con is the opposite: he acts like someone who thinks blind alleys and falsehoods do great damage and we need to do all we can to avoid them. He is *epistemically risk averse*. So, whereas Pro puts a higher value on acquiring true belief, Con puts a higher value on avoidance of false belief. Pro ends up living her life trying out new ideas and endorsing them even when the evidence isn't conclusive; Con ends up living his life withholding judgment until the evidence is overwhelming. Assuming they are comparable in general intelligence, curiosity, opportunities for thought, etc., Pro will probably acquire more true beliefs than Con, but Con will probably avoid more false beliefs than Pro. These tendencies just come naturally to them: they've never thought about any of this at all. We can sum this up by saying that they have different *starting points*: Pro naturally values "acquire truth" more than "avoid falsehood," whereas Con spontaneously does the opposite.

Now imagine that Pro and Con are on a jury deliberating on a defendant's guilt. Pro ends up thinking the defendant is guilty; Con thinks otherwise. They have the same evidence, they are equally intelligent, they have the same background knowledge, they think about the issue for the same amount of time under the same conditions, etc. Even so, Pro thinks the evidence is good enough to believe he's guilty; Con thinks the evidence isn't good enough to believe he's guilty. They merely have different ideas on how much evidence is enough for belief – although, as I mentioned earlier, none of this passes through their minds, as they confine their thoughts to the defendant's guilt (and don't think about epistemological matters such as "What is the proper amount of evidence here?").

Given the epistemic differences between them, Pro and Con might be epistemic peers on B and yet reasonably come to different conclusions regarding B's truth. Given that their starting points are different *and reasonable* – that's the key assumption here! – both of them end up with reasonable answers on the matter at hand even though they disagree. Pro judges the evidence to be good enough for belief; Con says it's not quite good enough. (In this case Con doesn't end up saying "B is false," but he does end up disagreeing with Pro in a sense, as Pro and Con hold different opinions on B, Pro saying it's true and Con withholding judgment.) This *might* be a counterexample to Uniqueness4.

Epistemologist Richard Feldman is aware of this kind of case. He questions whether we can safely assume that the two different background tendencies are reasonable, as I did in the second sentence of the previous paragraph (Feldman 2006). Sure, he would say, *if* both starting points are reasonable and yet differ enough to generate different conclusions (the conclusions: "I believe B" and "I suspend judgment on B"), *then* we can see how Pro's assenting to B and Con's withholding judgment from B can both be reasonable. Feldman questions whether the "if" is really true. It is clearly the case that not just *any* starting point will be reasonable: we can imagine people with bizarre cognitive tendencies that would not be reasonable (for example, if your tendency is to believe anything for which you have any evidence, even if the evidence is quite weak or you have loads of counterevidence as well). For my part, I wonder whether there is anything like the "right amount" of evidence one needs in order to believe something. It seems to me that there should be some significant wiggle room there. And if that's right, then I can see how two people who are "built" slightly differently, so to speak, might come to different yet reasonable verdicts concerning a given body of evidence.

So, for all those reasons, when we consider the question "Is Uniqueness true?," I am inclined to answer "No," although, as I mentioned several times, the discussion of these hard questions has really just begun.

Independence

There is another collection of key theoretical principles in the epistemology of disagreement. When you learn that so-and-so disagrees with you, and you had already come to the opinion that she was your peer or superior on the matter, then, when you're figuring out what to do with your belief B, you can't do anything like saying to yourself, "Well, since B is true and she says it's not true, she's made the error this time around; so I'll retain my belief." Instead, you must have some *other* reason for sticking with B. Reflections like this motivate two closely related principles.

> Negative Independence (NI): Suppose you believe B on the basis of reasons R. You also believe P/S, that so-and-so is your peer/superior on B. Then you come to acquire belief D, that so-and-so thinks B is false. In response to the disagreement, you retain B. If the retained belief/belief retention is epistemically reasonable, then in coming to retain B you needed *not* to rely on R.

> Positive Independence (PI): Suppose you believe B on the basis of reasons R. You also believe P/S, that so-and-so is your peer/superior on B. Then you come to acquire belief D, that so-and-so thinks B is false. In response to the disagreement, you retain B. If the retained belief/belief

retention is epistemically reasonable, then, in coming to retain B, you needed to have relied on some reasoning not involving R.

The conjunction of these principles says you have to do something in order to retain your belief reasonably (that's the "positive" point), but you can't do some things (that's the "negative" point). You need to have a good reason to keep your belief (that's PI), but this good reason can't involve your original reason for coming to believe B (that's NI). Instead, you need a *new reason* to keep B.

This is all pretty intuitive, I suppose, but perhaps only because we recognize that, in *paradigmatic cases of reasonable belief retention*, the person in question typically does have a good reason for keeping her belief and this good reason will be quite different from her original reason for B. For instance, she'll stick with B because she learns that her peer is drunk or terribly biased, and that's why he came to think B is false. However, I suspect that, in many cases of reasonable belief retention, neither NI nor PI is true.

In many of the stories in which the protagonist could reasonably retain B, what made her belief retention reasonable was the fact that it was caused by her implicit awareness that her evidence for B was much stronger than her evidence for P. However, she didn't need to be actually conscious of that: she didn't have to think to herself, "My evidence for the claim we disagree about is much stronger than my evidence for the idea that she's my peer on this matter." In real life we rarely have "meta" thoughts like that. All that matters to the reasonability of her belief retention is that she was *moved* to keep B by the disparity in evidence, regardless of whether she has any awareness that that is what's going on with her mind. If anyone had asked her what reasons she had for keeping B, she might not have anything intelligent to say. Most people are okay at reasoning, but they typically aren't good about reflecting on reasoning – their own or anyone else's. She might even be disposed to say something silly or unintelligent or irrelevant in response to our question "What reasons do you have for sticking with B?" – despite the fact that what made her keep B was entirely reasonable. So, things like that make me a little wary of PI.

Things are puzzling with regard to NI, which says that we can't rely on our original reasons for B. The question is this: when she keeps B because her evidence for B is much better than her evidence for P, is she "relying on her reasoning for B"? For what it's worth, it seems so to me, as it was that reasoning that made the evidence for B so good compared to that for P. If I'm right, then NI is false.

Conditional Peers and Superiors

In Part I we looked at two notions of peerhood: two people are peers on belief B when (i) they are equal on all Disagreement Factors or (ii) they are equally likely to judge B correctly. And those were the notions we used throughout the book. Epistemologists thinking about disagreement have looked at a third kind of peerhood, a "conditional" one in a sense I'll specify below.

Suppose I believe B, that global warming is happening. Suppose I also believe P, that Nathan is my peer regarding B in this sense: I think we are equally likely to judge B correctly. I have this opinion of Nathan because I figure that he knows about as well as I do the basic facts about expert consensus, he understands and respects that consensus about as much as I do, and he based his opinion of B on those facts. (I know he has some opinion on B but I don't yet know what it is.) So, in one sense, I think he is my peer on B. Let's say that *I think you're my O-peer on B* = I think we are equally likely to judge B's truth-value correctly. "O" is for "ordinary," since this is an ordinary notion of peerhood (ordinary for real life). This is the *likelihood* notion we have been operating with.

But in another sense I don't think he is my peer on B. After all, if someone asked me, "Suppose you find out later today that Nathan sincerely thinks B is false. What do you think are the odds that you'll be right and he'll be wrong about B?" I would reply with "Over 95 percent!" I would answer that way because I'm *very* confident in B's truth and, if I find out that Nathan disagrees with that idea, I will be quite confident that he's wrong and I'm right. So in that sense I think I have a *definite epistemic advantage over him*: given how confident I am in B, I think that, if it turns out we disagree over B, there is a 95 percent chance I'm right and he's wrong. (Of course, given that I think that we are equally likely to judge B correctly and I'm very confident in B, I'm also very confident that he will judge B to be true; so, when I'm asked to think about the possibility that Nathan thinks B is false, I think I'm being asked to consider a very unlikely scenario. But the important point here is this: if I have the view that, if it turns out that he really thinks B is false, the odds that I'm right and he's wrong are 95 percent, then in a real sense my view is that he's not "fully" my peer on B, as I think that when it comes to the possibility of disagreement I'm very confident that I will be in the right and he won't be.

Now consider this case, which is very different.

54 Conditional Peers

Suppose we are the same age and take all the same math and science classes through high school. We're both moderately good at math. In fact, we almost always get the same grades. On many occasions we come up with different answers for homework problems. As far as we have been able to determine, in those cases 30 percent of the time I've been right, 30 percent of the time you've been right, and 40 percent of the time we've both been wrong. Suppose I know this interesting fact about our track records! Now we are in college together. I will believe, on the basis of our track records, that, on the next math problem we happen to disagree about, the odds that my answer is right equals the odds that your answer is right – unless there is some reason to think one of us has some advantage in this particular case (e.g., I've had a lot more time to work on it, or some other significant discrepancy in Disagreement Factors). Suppose further that, on the next typical math problem we work on, I think that neither of us has any advantage over the other this time around. And then I find out that you got an answer different from mine.

In this math case I first come to think that B (my answer) is true. But I also think that, if I were to discover that you think B is false, the odds that I'm right and you're wrong are equal to the odds that I'm wrong and you're right. That's very different from the global warming case, in which I think that, if I were to discover that you think B is false, the odds that I'm right and you're wrong are nineteen times the odds that I'm wrong and you're right (95 percent is nineteen times 5 percent).

Let's say that *I think you're my C-peer on B* = before I find out your view on B, but after I have come to believe B, I think that *if* it turns out that you disbelieve B, *then* the chance that I'm right about B is equal to the chance that you're right about B. "C" is for "conditional": sentences of the form "If this, then that" are called *conditionals* in philosophy and logic, and this notion of peerhood centers on a conditional. So, although I think Nathan is my O-peer on the global warming belief, I don't think he is my C-peer on that belief. I think he is my C-inferior on that matter. But in the math case I thought you were my O-peer *and* my C-peer on the relevant belief.

When investigating the notion of C-peerhood, it is important to think about the *likelihood in real life* that you will have decent evidence that someone is your C-peer on some important issue. Wouldn't you have to know someone incredibly well to have any good evidence that she is your C-peer with respect to some interesting claim? That's what the Conditional Peers story suggests. With most any real case of recognized disagreement involving some claim of importance, one will have precious little evidence or even confidence that someone is one's C-peer – in fact, in my experience people have difficulty even *grasping* the concept of a C-peer, which suggests that they have no opinions about such matters in cases of disagreement. For those reasons I'm skeptical that the C-peerhood holds much import for real-life disagreements.

Waiving that practical consideration, there remains the question of what is the reasonable thing for me to do in the math story when I discover that you think B is false (whereas I had already concluded that B is true)? What should you do when you discover that you disagree with someone you took to be a C-peer? I will not investigate that question in this book.

Feldman's Questions

Now I'd like to address some of the key questions raised by Richard Feldman, since they have influenced professional discussions and Feldman introduces some useful terminology.

Suppose, as before, that Pro believes B and Con believes not-B, although neither person knows anything about the other. As a matter of fact they are epistemic peers regarding B: they have seen just about the same evidence, they are about equal in relevant intelligence, they are about equal in relevant bias, they have considered B for about the same length of time and with about the same care, etc. We can stipulate that Pro and Con are equal in *all* the Disagreement Factors. Feldman asks the following question.

F1: Is Pro's belief B and Con's belief not-B reasonable before they find out about any disagreement?

If the answer to F1 is "Yes," then, in Feldman's terminology, there can be *reasonable disagreements in isolation*. This is just the question of whether Uniqueness1 is false, with the implicit proviso that the two people are equal in all Disagreement Factors, not just evidence. As I explained above in the discussion of Uniqueness, there is reason to think the answer to F1 is "Yes."

Next, Pro learns about Con. She comes to know that she and Con are epistemic peers concerning the topics relevant to B. She thinks to herself: "He's just as likely as I am to come to the right opinion regarding B." At this point she doesn't know Con's view on B. Similarly, Con comes to know about Pro and comes to think that she is just as likely as he is to come to the right opinion on B. And Con doesn't yet know what Pro thinks about B.

Then Pro learns that Con thinks B is false and Con learns that Pro thinks B is true. But they have yet to share their reasons with each other. The next thing they'll do is talk to each other, discussing their reasons for their opposing views. So suppose Pro tells Con her reasons for thinking B is true and Con tells Pro his reasons for thinking B is false. They discuss those reasons at length. This discussion, in which they fully share their reasons behind their differing views on B, might take five minutes, it might take five weeks, it might take five years; it all depends on how difficult it is and how involved their reasons are. This point in the process is called *after full disclosure*, as they have fully disclosed to each other their reasons for their opinions on B *and* they know that they have shared all their reasons.

It turns out that, after all that discussion, Pro still thinks B is true and Con still thinks B is false. In fact, they are just as confident in their opinions as when they started out. So they have not lowered their confidence levels concerning B. I assume that you have experienced disagreements that fit this pattern.

Feldman's discussion motivates two more questions:

F2: Are both of their actions of not changing their views on belief B reasonable after full disclosure?

F3: Are their retained B and not-B beliefs both reasonable after full disclosure?

Feldman would answer both of them with "No," although he explicitly treats just F3. If the answer to F3 is "Yes," then, in Feldman's terminology, there can be *reasonable disagreements after full disclosure*. It isn't hard to see how intuitive Feldman's judgment is. If you know full well that you have shared *all* your evidence for your judgment that B is true, and you know full well that the other person is *just as likely as you* are to judge that evidence accurately, and then you find out that they disagree with you, how on earth can you have any reason to favor your view over hers?

Well, let's think about it. During the full disclosure process Pro will come to learn the reason(s) R that Con has for rejecting B. There are two possibilities regarding how Pro will react to this information: she may think Con's total reason R for not-B is a significant one that she hadn't taken account of before, or she may think Con's R isn't a significant one that she hadn't already encountered. If the former, then Pro will either suspend judgment on B or switch to disbelieving it: after all, *by her own lights* she's been presented with excellent evidence against her former belief, evidence she never knew about and that she judges to be comparable in strength to her evidence for her belief. If the latter, then she will stick with her belief in B and probably come to the conclusion that Con is not really her peer on B. In that case, Pro will consider the reason R that Con has for not-B and judge that R just doesn't support not-B that much. In all probability, she will not think that Con is her peer when it comes to R even if she did so judge regarding B: just because she thought that Con was her peer on B doesn't mean that she thought that he was her peer on R as well. She could reasonably say to herself, "Well, Con thinks R shows that B is false. Although there's nothing stupid with that view, Con's just wrong to think R shows anything like that." (It's interesting to consider the admittedly rare case in which Pro does think that Con is her peer on R as well as B; what happens then?) Now, Pro might be wrong in this judgment that R isn't a good reason for not-B (more exactly: the judgment that it doesn't provide her a good reason for giving up her belief B). But being wrong doesn't necessarily mean being unreasonable.

Moreover, and as we have seen several times, if the shared pot of evidence is complicated enough (e.g., the split experts cases), it might be the case that, even after a thorough sharing of evidence, the discussants might reasonably disagree on what the shared evidence says. Perhaps in cases of complicated evidence the two people can't "fully" disclose their evidence. Feldman doesn't define the notion with precision. In any case, the complicated evidence cases supply some more reason to suspect the answer to F2 and F3 is "Yes." The argument regarding "starting points" (from our discussion of Uniqueness) does the same thing.

Feldman has one more interesting question for us to consider. As described above, Pro has stuck with her belief B in the face of her disagreement with Con; similarly, Con has kept his belief not-B. Pro thinks that Con has made an error regarding B, but let's suppose that she also thinks that Con's retained view that B is false is reasonable even though it's false. Further, Con thinks Pro's continued belief in B is reasonable. Pro might be a philosopher who thinks we have free will; her colleague thinks otherwise; but they consider they are peers on the issue and they *also* think that *both* of them are reasonable in retaining their contrary beliefs. Pro disagrees with Con, but she thinks his belief and his reasoning for it is highly intelligent and rational.

Actually, I think this set-up is unrealistic: the notion of peerhood would have to be very lax in order to have much application to real life – especially when it comes to the complex beliefs we care about most, such as religious, moral, and political ones. It is common for someone to know that there are people who disagree with her and who are, in her judgment, being quite reasonable. That's fine. What is rare, I think, is the idea that she will consider that they are her peers regarding the belief in question. Pro will hardly have any good reason to think her colleague Con has the same evidence she does regarding the question of free will, even under an approximate notion of peerhood. We saw this point in the discussion of religious disagreement, but it applies to the vast majority of our political, moral, and philosophical beliefs as well.

In any case, we have Feldman's final question: are we being reasonable when we say of someone we take to be our peer on B, "Well, I disagree with him about B, but his view is reasonable"? Feldman isn't asking whether Pro's belief in Con's reasonability is *true*; he's asking if Pro's attitude regarding Con is a reasonable one *for Pro to have*. More generally:

> F4: Is Pro's belief "Con's belief in not-B is reasonable even though it's false" reasonable after full disclosure (and we ask the same of Con's belief in Pro's reasonableness)?

If the answer to F4 is "Yes," then, in Feldman's terminology, there can be *mutually recognized reasonable disagreements*. Feldman says the answer is "No." There is reason to think Feldman is right. To see this, put yourself in Pro's position. You have considered a body of evidence regarding B. You have come to think that it shows B is true. That's your judgment on the matter. And now you've shared all your evidence with Con; and Con has shared all his evidence with you; and yet Con still says that B is false. So you are now saying that Con has fouled up, has made a mistake: whereas the fact (according to you) is that the evidence shows B is true, Con has looked at the same body of evidence and said that it shows that B is false. Aren't you going to think that he is being unreasonable here, since he has the evidence in front of him and has misjudged it (and he had the same amount of time as you to think about it; remember that there are multiple Disagreement Factors)? By sharing your evidence you have grown much more confident in P than before; so, even if you started out a lot more confident in B than in P, that's no longer true. Nor is it true that you are more confident in B than in D: the long discussion in which you shared your evidence will increase your confidence that the two of you genuinely disagree. So the obvious ways of being reasonable in keeping B will no longer apply.

I'm not going to give any arguments, pro or con, regarding F4 (beyond the clarificatory one in the previous paragraph). Instead, let's just look at some interpretive questions. When Pro says that Con's belief not-B is reasonable, does she mean that it's *optimally* reasonable? Does she mean that Con's belief is *just as reasonable* as her belief B? Or is it something else? And is Feldman asking whether Pro's belief about Con's belief is optimally reasonable or something else? Finally, in ordinary life, what concept(s) do people actually express when they say things such as "I think he's wrong, but his position is reasonable"?

10
The Disagreement Question Revisited

Finally, we have the Disagreement Question to tackle. I'm not going to do it: I'm going to leave you hanging in suspense. But I will get the ball rolling by suggesting how to proceed.

Suppose Jack thinks Jill is his peer (or even superior) when it comes to belief B. He also thinks B is true. Then he hears Jill say that she thinks B is false. Suppose further that he retains his belief in B. Under what conditions is his belief retention reasonable assuming he sticks with his belief in B?

There are just three answers that are even in the running for serious consideration.

> View 1: It is never reasonable. He has to suspend judgment on B in all cases.

> View 2: It is reasonable in some but not all cases. He has to suspend judgment on B in just some cases, as he can reasonably retain B provided a certain condition C holds (and then we have to figure out what C is; see below).

> View 3: It is always reasonable. He can keep B in all cases.

We have already seen good reasons to reject views 1 and 3. In section 2 we saw several stories in which one is reasonable in keeping B; so view 1 is out. The Restaurant Bill I story suffices to show that view 3 is out. (And no doubt you could think of many other stories that refute view 3.) So, the truth must lie with view 2. For different Cs we end up with different proposals. Here is a highly arbitrary list of ten of them:

1   Your belief retention is reasonable = You know B.
2   Your belief retention is reasonable = You know B and you know D.
3   Your belief retention is reasonable = You know B and you believe but don't know P.
4   Your belief retention is reasonable = You know B, you know D, and you believe but don't know P.
5   Your belief retention is reasonable = Your overall evidence for B is excellent.
6   Your belief retention is reasonable = Your overall evidence for B is much better than your overall evidence for P.
7   Your belief retention is reasonable = Your overall evidence for B and for P is much better than your overall evidence for D.
8   Your belief retention is reasonable = You have a good reason independent of the debate over B to favor your own position.
9   Your belief retention is reasonable = Your overall evidence for B is much stronger than the evidence against B supplied by your beliefs P and D.
10 Your belief retention is reasonable = Your confidence in B is much stronger than your confidence in either P or D.

There is nothing central about (1) to (10). As you can imagine, one could easily fiddle around with them to generate another ten proposals (and then another ten, and then yet another ten . . .). An excellent exercise is this: take the stories we have gone over in Part II and see how the above proposals fare when applied to them – and do the same for the proposals one finds in the professional literature.

Although we haven't paid much attention to the epistemic state *knowledge*, it's not hard to think of cases that put pressure on (1) to (4). Here is one that gets the ball rolling (although it doesn't *refute* (1) to (4)):

55   Name Conspiracy

Right now you *know* what your name is. But imagine that, starting tomorrow, you unknowingly encountered an odd conspiracy meant to fool you into thinking that your real name is different. Your parents tell you that your real name is "Chris". They show you (fake) documents that seem to prove it: birth certificates, hospital records, tax forms, social security forms, etc. They also offer a reasonable explanation as to why they lied to you about your first name. Assume further that your parents are not the type of people who ever play practical jokes, forge documents, or anything like that. If you like, pile more material on to the story: you go to the official records office in your home state and the person behind the counter (who is part of the conspiracy) confirms your parents' story, etc.

Even though right now, as you read this book, you do indeed know your name (I'm assuming that a general kind of radical skepticism about knowledge is false and your situation vis-à-vis your name is typical), if all this happened to you in the future, then you would be unreasonable to stick with your belief in your name. Hence, knowledge doesn't guarantee reasonableness in retaining that knowledge. In addition, we could add to many of our stories the stipulation that the protagonist knew B before the discovery of disagreement.

11

Concluding Thoughts: Does Disagreement Require Suspending Judgment in Important Cases?

We have seen that there are many situations in which one is reasonable in keeping one's old belief B even when aware of lots of disagreeing peers or superiors. In brief, we saw good reason to think one can reasonably retain one's beliefs when something akin to any of the following conditions holds:

> If you believe that the people who agree with you are in a much better position to judge belief B correctly than the people who disagree with you, then you're reasonable in retaining B.

> If you hold controversial belief B, you become convinced that lots of intelligent people you respect believe not-B (where you believe that some of these people are your peers while others are your superiors or inferiors), but you also come to think that the experts taken as a large group definitely agree with you, then you are reasonable if you stick with your belief B.

> If you believe P, which is the claim that the people who disagree with you are about as well positioned to judge belief B correctly as the people who agree with you, but you are much more confident in B than in P, then retaining B will be reasonable.

If you believe S, that the group you're disagreeing with is in a better position (but not extremely so) than your group (the group of people who believe B) to judge belief B correctly, but you are much more confident in B than in S, then your retaining B will be reasonable.

It is tempting to think that that means we can stick to our guns in a great many real-life situations. And, if that's true, then perhaps we haven't learned anything in this book that will mean we have to adjust our lives when encountering disagreement.

I don't think so, for three reasons. The first is simple: just because keeping one's belief is reasonable doesn't mean that the retained belief is reasonable. We saw this in section 11 of Part I. Second, and more important, the real question to face at this point is this: can we reasonably stick to our guns when it comes to *our most cherished beliefs* – the ones that we really care about and that may even give our lives direction? For most readers, some but not all of the following beliefs are quite important:

a) God loves me.
b) God hears me.
c) There is no God.
d) My wife/husband/partner really loves me.
e) Politician Pat is really working hard on our behalf.
f) I am basically a good, moral person.
g) My parents love me.
h) There is an afterlife.
i) There is no afterlife.
j) I'm going to do just fine after I graduate.
k) I'm good at sex.
l) My country is basically just.
m) I was right to yell at him; he deserved it.
n) I don't *have* to give money to beggars on the street.
o) I'm smarter than they are.
p) I'm better at my job than most of my co-workers/colleagues.

I chose those beliefs because we typically hold them with *high confidence* and would experience *great discomfort* if we found out that the beliefs were false or even that there really wasn't any good evidence for them. If you grew up in the USA, then you are probably very confident that William Howard Taft was a US president a long time ago. If you found out you were wrong, you would be surprised but it probably wouldn't upset you too much. You would be annoyed that your memory was so bad, but that's about it. On the other hand, if you were convinced that there was a divine afterlife and then found out that the evidence concerning that idea not only wasn't supportive but strongly went against your belief, then you might be *shaken*. All of a sudden your religious faith might be turned upside down. The same holds for the reverse belief: if you have long been convinced that there is no afterlife, and then you learned that there was very impressive evidence that there really is an afterlife, you might be staggered: the question "What is going to happen to me after I die?" might immediately become profoundly important to you.

The phenomenon of disagreement supplies a *skeptical threat*: for many of our cherished beliefs, if we aren't sheltered, then we know that there is a great deal of controversy about those beliefs even among the people who have worked the hardest and smartest in trying to figure out whether they are really true; but to retain a belief in the face of that kind of controversy is irrational; and a belief that is irrational does not amount to knowledge; thus, our beliefs we recognize as controversial do not amount to knowledge.[12] This conclusion is a form of philosophical skepticism. It says we have to suspend judgment on a great many of our important beliefs.

For the sake of argument I will assume that controversial beliefs very often *start out* epistemically rational and even overall justified (in any of several senses of those terms). Roughly put, the disagreement skeptic thinks that, even if a controversial belief starts out as knowledge, once one appreciates the controversy, one's belief will *no longer* amount to knowledge. The disagreement skeptic focuses on beliefs that satisfy the following recognition-of-controversy conditions.

[12] This and the next few paragraphs draw on my "Skepticism and Disagreement", forthcoming in Diego Machuca and Baron Reed (eds), *Skepticism: From Antiquity to the Present*, Bloomsbury.

You know that the belief B in question has been investigated and debated (i) for a very long time by (ii) a great many (iii) very smart people who (iv) are your epistemic superiors on the matter and (v) have worked very hard (vi) under optimal circumstances to figure out if B is true. But you also know that (vii) these experts have not come to any significant agreement on B and (viii) those who agree with you are not, as a group, in a better position to judge B than those who disagree with you.

We typically come to know (i) to (viii) through testimony; the truths known are just brute facts about society of which we are well aware. For instance, I might have some opinion regarding free will or capital punishment or affirmative action or spiritual experience or the causes of World War II. I know full well that these matters have been debated by an enormous number of really smart people for a very long time – in some cases, for centuries. I also know that I'm no expert and that there are genuine experts on those topics – at least, they have thought about those topics *much* longer than I have, with a great deal more awareness of relevant considerations, etc. It's no contest: I know I'm just an amateur compared to them. Part of being reflective is coming to know about your comparative epistemic status on controversial subjects.

The person who knows (i) to (viii) is robbed of the reasonableness of several comforting responses to the discovery of controversy. If she is reasonable, then she realizes that she can't make, at least with confidence, anything like the following remarks:

- Well, the people who agree with me are smarter than the people who disagree with me.
- We have crucial evidence they don't have.
- We have studied the key issue a great deal more than they have.
- They are a lot more biased than we are.

This phenomenon is particularly prevalent with regard to religion, politics, morality, and philosophy. To see why, recall college student Stu from the Group Projects stories. When he learned that the other group disagreed with him, he could reasonably say to himself, "Well, I guess they didn't do as much work on the issue as I thought," or "Maybe they aren't as smart as I thought," or "Perhaps they just screwed up the count of the states that allow gay marriage or made some other slip, even though they're just as generally smart and thorough as we are." But when it comes to debates about free will, capital punishment, affirmative action, and many other standard controversial topics, a great many of us – not all of us, but many – either know that such responses are false or we embrace them irrationally. If, when it comes to the question of whether we have free will, you say to yourself, regarding the experts who disagree with you, "Those people just don't understand the issues," "They aren't very smart," "They haven't thought about it much," etc., then you are doing so irrationally in the sense that *you should know better* than to say that, at least if you're honest with yourself and informed of the state of the debate over free will.

This will apply to many beliefs from our list, such as (a), (b), (c), (e), (h), (i), and (l). So there is a real threat of skepticism for those beliefs: even if the controversial belief is true, it won't amount to knowledge.

However, this connection between controversy and skepticism won't apply to many of the other beliefs in the list: the odds are, it won't apply to at least (d), (f), (g), (j), (k), (m), and (n). No one (or no one you know) is going around saying your parents don't love you, you aren't a basically moral person, you stink at sex, etc. So those beliefs are probably immune to any skeptical argument of the form "There is long-standing disagreement among experts regarding your belief B; you know all about it (viz. conditions (i) to (viii)); you have no good reason to discount the ones who disagree with you; so, you shouldn't retain your belief B."

However, at least for me, this is cold comfort, which leads to my third point in this section. Once I started worrying about disagreement I started thinking about *other* uncomfortable issues that put pressure on my beliefs – including ones like those that escape the controversy-skepticism line of reasoning. I assume I am not atypical. Once we ask ourselves a question such as this:

Do I really have any reason to think the people I agree with are in a better position to judge this issue than the people we disagree with?

We end up asking questions such as these:

> Do I have any real reason to think I'm above average at work, as a driver, as a partner, as a parent, as a son? Or am I thinking those things just because they are flattering for me?
>
> Is there any objective reason to think my political views are worth a damn, given that I don't even really follow politics that much compared to others?

And those questions generate more general and troubling ones:

> How often are my important beliefs based on evidence anyway? Maybe my genes are the primary factor behind what I end up believing. Or maybe I'm guilty of wishful thinking a lot more than I used to think (e.g., maybe I believe in God just because it's convenient or comforting). Or maybe I'm just a sheep, blindly following what my culture says (e.g., that capitalism is a good idea).
>
> Upon realizing that so many people disagree with me I also vividly become aware of the vast amount of evidence that is directly relevant to my belief but which I know nothing about. For instance, I may have some view about capital punishment or affirmative action or religion or free will. I applaud myself because I know I've thought long and hard before coming to my view on the matter. But then I realize that the bit of evidence I looked at is minuscule compared to what's out there. All I have to do is go to the library and see row upon row of books on the topics to know that there is oodles of evidence out there that I know nothing about. Why should I think that the tiny portion of evidence on which I based my opinion is really any good?

And, because it ends up difficult to supply any honest answers that reflect happily on myself, I start to wonder whether my comforting but uncontroversial beliefs are really true.

12
Study Questions
and Problems

Many of the study questions in the final section of Part I had definite answers. Most of the ones below are harder, requiring careful reflection.

> *Problem 1:* Go through all of Part II and list the primary lessons of each story. This will take a long time, but completing this task is probably the most valuable thing you could do towards mastering the material.

> *Problem 2:* We looked at cases in which one's evidence for B far exceeded one's evidence for P. In those cases it seemed as though the reasonable thing to do is to keep B. But what if we *iterate* the disagreements? First you run into subject S1 who disagrees with B; you stick with B because your evidence for B is significantly better than your evidence for P1 (P1 = "S1 is my peer on B"). Second, you run into subject S2 who disagrees with B; you retain B because your evidence for B is significantly better than your evidence for P2. Suppose this happens a thousand more times. In some cases, this iteration should not give you any significant new evidence regarding B; in others it does. Come up with stories that illustrate the differences.

> *Problem 3:* In many stories we have said things such as "The reasonable thing to do is stick with B" or "The reasonable thing to do is suspend judgment on B." But when we say things like this, are we saying that the person in question is *permitted* to stick with or suspend judgment on B? Or are we saying that she is *required* to stick with

or suspend judgment on B? (The permitted/required distinction is important in life. For instance, at a certain intersection you are permitted but not required to turn right; but you are both permitted and required to stop.) Look at a variety of our stories in order to answer the question.

Problem 4: For some stories we said that, if the person's evidence for B is much better than her evidence for P, then she is reasonable in sticking with B. But, in order for her reasonably to stick with B, does she actually have to say to herself anything along the lines of, "Well, my reasons for B are a lot better than my reasons for P; so I'll keep B"? In other words, is the mere brute fact that her evidence for B is better than her evidence for P enough to secure the reasonableness of her belief retention even if she is unaware of that fact? Or does she need to be aware, at least implicitly, that her evidence for B is much better than her evidence for P?

Problem 5: In the Quad story the protagonist was befuddled: she was totally confident in B and totally confident in P, but then her colleague insisted that B was false. This shows how difficult it is to find a case where one can be reasonable in being 100 percent confident in B, P, *and* D. Try to think of a story in which this happens. Perhaps the protagonist in your story will end up thinking that her peer has made a performance error. Accordingly, try to come up with another story – one in which the protagonist is 100 percent confident in B, P, and D, *and* "Neither I nor my peer made a performance error."

Problem 6: Rewrite the Decision Procedure from section 1 so as to accommodate the alleged insights gained in Part II.

Problem 7: People often don't follow their evidence. For instance, their overall evidence regarding B dictates that they should not accept B but they go ahead and accept B anyway. Here are three main types of situation in which someone fails to follow her evidence:

a)   She doesn't know what her overall evidence says. And then wishful thinking, for example, causes her to go in the opposite direction to what her evidence says.

b)   She honestly thinks her evidence says one thing when in fact it says the opposite.

c)   She knows which way her evidence points, but because of intellectual weakness she ignores it and believes the opposite.

Do two things. First, come up with your own stories that illustrate each of (a) to (c). Second, figure out whether there are other ways of not following one's evidence. If there are, describe them.

Problem 8: Try to come up with an equation like those considered in section 10 – one that isn't refuted by any of the stories in Part II. You might want to start with the *** rules.

Problem 9: Some philosophers want to dig in their heels and reject a good portion of the arguments in Part II – especially those in section 2. They want to say something like this: if you truly *know* B, then there just has to be something epistemically wrong with suspending judgment on B in reaction to the discovery of disagreement. The Name Conspiracy story seems to refute the most extreme of these views. Still, it's not hard to get into a frame of mind in which it seems that the whole point of inquiry is the attaining of knowledge; and, if that's so, it suggests that (a) there's always something epistemically seriously wrong with suspending judgment when one initially had knowledge and (b) there's always something epistemically right with keeping with knowledge come what may. Assess (a) and (b).

Guide to Further Reading

After studying this book, you have several key places to go for further readings. It would probably be a good idea to begin with the works that started the topic off in the first two years:

Feldman, Richard (2006) "Epistemological Puzzles about Disagreement," in *Epistemology Futures*, ed. Stephen Hetherington, Oxford University Press.

Frances, Bryan (2005) "When a Skeptical Hypothesis is Live," *Noûs* 39: 559–95.

Frances, Bryan (2005) *Scepticism Comes Alive*, Oxford University Press.

Kelly, Thomas (2006) "The Epistemic Significance of Disagreement," in *Oxford Studies in Epistemology*, 1, ed. John Hawthorne and Tamar Gendler Szabo, Oxford University Press: 167–96.

And then proceed to the next "wave" of key works, appearing over the next three years:

Christensen, David (2007) "Epistemology of Disagreement: the Good News," *Philosophical Review* 116: 187–217.

Elga, Adam (2007) "Reflection and Disagreement," *Noûs* 41: 478–502.

Feldman, Richard (2007) "Reasonable Religious Disagreements," in *Philosophers without Gods: Meditations on Atheism and the Secular Life*, ed. Louise Antony, Oxford University Press: 194–214.

Goldberg, Sanford (2009) "Reliabilism in Philosophy," *Philosophical Studies* 142: 105–17.

Kelly, Thomas (2008) "Disagreement, Dogmatism, and Belief Polarization," *Journal of Philosophy* 105: 611–33.

Lackey, Jennifer (2008) "A Justificationist View of Disagreement's Epistemic Significance," in *Social Epistemology*, ed. Alan Millar,

Adrian Haddock, and Duncan Pritchard, Oxford University Press: 298–325.

Lackey, Jennifer (2008) "What Should We Do When We Disagree?" in *Oxford Studies in Epistemology*, ed. Tamar Szabó Gendler and John Hawthorne, Oxford University Press: 274–93.

In addition, there are the two books mentioned earlier:

Feldman, Richard, and Ted Warfield, eds (2010) *Disagreement*, Oxford University Press.

Lackey, Jennifer, and David Christensen, eds (2013) *The Epistemology of Disagreement: New Essays*, Oxford University Press.

A 2009 edition of the journal *Episteme* (vol. 6, no. 3) is an excellent source as well, since it is devoted entirely to the epistemology of disagreement.

A few people have written introductions to the topic:

Christensen, David (2009) "Disagreement as Evidence: The Epistemology of Controversy," *Philosophy Compass* 4: 756–67.

Frances, Bryan (2010) "Disagreement," in *Routledge Companion to Epistemology*, ed. Duncan Pritchard and Sven Bernecker, Routledge: 68–74.

Frances, Bryan, and Nathan Ballantyne (forthcoming) "Disagreement," in the online *Stanford Encyclopedia of Philosophy*.

An especially interesting subtopic is *religious disagreement*, as briefly discussed in section 7 of Part II. Here are some works on that subtopic:

Bogardus, Tomás (2013) "Disagreeing with the (Religious) Skeptic," *International Journal for Philosophy of Religion* 74: 5–17.

DePoe, John (2011) "The Significance of Religious Disagreement," in *Taking Christian Moral Thought Seriously: The Legitimacy of Christian Thought in the Marketplace of Ideas*, ed. Jeremy Evans, Nashville: Broadman & Holman Academic: 48–76.

Frances, Bryan (forthcoming, 2014) "Religious Disagreement," in *Handbook of Contemporary Philosophy of Religion*, ed. Graham Oppy, Acumen Press.

King, Nathan L. (2008) "Religious Diversity and its Challenges to Religious Belief," *Philosophy Compass* 3: 830–53.

Kraft, James (2012) *The Epistemology of Religious Disagreement: A Better Understanding*, Palgrave Macmillan.

Lackey, Jennifer (2014) "Taking Religious Disagreement Seriously," in *Religious Faith and Intellectual Virtue*, ed. Timothy O'Connor and Laura Frances Goins, Oxford University Press.

Leech, David, and Aku Visala (2012) "Naturalistic Explanation for Religious Belief," *Philosophy Compass* 7: 552–63.

McKim, Robert (2001) *Religious Ambiguity and Religious Diversity*, Oxford University Press.

Oppy, Graham (2010) "Disagreement," *International Journal for Philosophy of Religion* 68: 183–99.

Thune, Michael (2011) "Religious Belief and the Epistemology of Disagreement," *Philosophy Compass* 6: 712–24.

An excellent article on both religious and other controversial kinds of disagreement is by one of the best thinkers on the epistemology of disagreement:

Christensen, David (forthcoming) "Disagreement and Public Controversy," in *Essays in Collective Epistemology*, ed. Jennifer Lackey, Oxford University Press.

A more comprehensive and constantly updated bibliography can be found under the heading "Epistemology of Disagreement" on the PhilPapers website, at http://philpapers.org/browse/epistemology-of-disagreement. For what it's worth, here are some of my recommendations on other works (not included above) worth studying:

Ballantyne, Nathan (forthcoming) "Counterfactual Philosophers," *Philosophy and Phenomenological Research*.

Boyce, Kenneth, and Allan Hazlett (n.d.) "Multi-Peer Disagreement and the Preface Paradox," unpublished MS, at www.philosophy.ed.ac.uk/people/view.php?name=allan-hazlett.

Christensen, David (2010) "Higher-Order Evidence," *Philosophy and Phenomenological Research* 81: 185–215.

Christensen, David (2011) "Disagreement, Question-Begging, and Epistemic Self-Criticism," *Philosophers' Imprint* 11: 1–22.

Decker, Jason (2012) "Disagreement, Evidence, and Agnosticism," *Synthese* 187: 753–83.

Enoch, David (2010) "Not Just a Truthometer: Taking Oneself Seriously (but Not Too Seriously) in Cases of Peer Disagreement," *Mind* 119: 953–97.

Frances, Bryan (2008) "Spirituality, Expertise, and Philosophers," in *Oxford Studies in Philosophy of Religion*, ed. Jon Kvanvig, Oxford University Press.

Frances, Bryan (2010) "The Reflective Epistemic Renegade," *Philosophy and Phenomenological Research* 81: 419–63.

Frances, Bryan (2012) "Discovering Disagreeing Epistemic Peers and Superiors," *International Journal of Philosophical Studies* 20: 1–21.

Hazlett, Allan (2012) "Higher-Order Epistemic Attitudes and Intellectual Humility," *Episteme* 9: 205–23.

Hazlett, Allan (forthcoming) "Entitlement and Mutually Recognized Reasonable Disagreement," *Episteme*.

King, Nathan L. (2012) "Disagreement: What's the Problem? Or A Good Peer is Hard to Find," *Philosophy and Phenomenological Research* 85: 249–72.

Lam, Barry (2011) "On the Rationality of Belief-Invariance in Light of Peer Disagreement," *Philosophical Review* 120: 207–45.

Lasonen-Aarnio, Maria (2013) "Disagreement and Evidential Attenuation," *Noûs* 47: 767–94.

Machuca, Diego, ed. (2013) *Disagreement and Skepticism*, Routledge.

Matheson, Jonathan (2011) "The Case for Rational Uniqueness," *Logic and Episteme* 2: 359–73.

Pettit, Philip (2006) "When to Defer to Majority Testimony – and When Not," *Analysis* 66: 179–87.

Ribeiro, Brian (2011) "Philosophy and Disagreement," *Crítica* 43: 3–25.

Rotondo, Andrew (2013) "Undermining, Circularity, and Disagreement," *Synthese* 190: 563–84.

Simpson, Robert Mark (2013) "Epistemic Peerhood and the Epistemology of Disagreement," *Philosophical Studies* 164: 561–77.

Thune, Michael (2010) " 'Partial Defeaters' and the Epistemology of Disagreement," *Philosophical Quarterly* 60: 355–72.

Wietmarschen, Han van (2013) "Peer Disagreement, Evidence, and Well-Groundedness," *Philosophical Review* 122: 395–425.

Index